FIRSTS, LASTS
& ONLYS®

TENNIS

FIRSTS, LASTS
& ONLYS®

TENNIS

A TRULY WONDERFUL COLLECTION
OF TENNIS TRIVIA

PAUL DONNELLEY

First published by Pitch Publishing, 2020

Pitch Publishing
A2 Yeoman Gate
Yeoman Way
Worthing
Sussex
BN13 3QZ
www.pitchpublishing.co.uk
info@pitchpublishing.co.uk

A CIP catalogue record is available for this book
from the British Library.

ISBN 978 1 78531 636 4

Typesetting and origination by Pitch Publishing

Printed and bound in UK by TJ International Ltd.

THE FIRSTS

THE LASTS

THE ONLYS

Dedication

For Sutchi, his wife, Sasha, and their two sons, Sultan and Snow. Oh, and the Serious Girl, *naturellement*.

Introduction and Acknowledegments

This is the fifth in the *Firsts, Lasts & Onlys*® sport series, coming after cricket, football, golf and rugby.

It is not intended to be a comprehensive tennis encyclopaedia but an enjoyable romp through one of the world's most exciting sports.

I like the facts, the trivia, the minutiae of life and this book on tennis is no different. Where else would you find out when chairs were first provided for players (surprisingly late), who is the only player to do a Grand Slam twice, what a Golden Slam is or what Boris Becker described as "the most expensive five seconds" of his life?

Two tennis players survived the sinking of *Titanic*, while later in the same century, one was asked not to turn up in a white Lycra bodysuit. All life is indeed here. I hope you enjoy.

I would like to thank the following for help, inspiration and kindness: the late and still much missed Jeremy Beadle, who was always endlessly encouraging; my agent Chelsey Fox, coming up to 25 years; my patient publisher Jane Camillin – this is our sixth book together and one day, I promise, I will deliver the manuscript on time; Duncan Olner, who designed the book cover; thanks also to the eagle-eyed Andrea Dunn for her expert proof-reading. Her excellence saved me from a number of errors; Larissa Kleine from the press office at Owl Arena; Dr Alex May of the *Oxford Dictionary of National Biography*; Mitchell Symons. And those people who have supported my books in the past: Rory Bremner, Piers Morgan, Richard Littlejohn, Dickie Bird, Frank McLintock, the late Michael Winner and the late Bob Monkhouse.

Paul Donnelley
Essex, 2020
www.pauldonnelley.com

The author

Paul Donnelley is the author of 29 books on a variety of subjects including sport, true crime, films, television, scandal, music and cars.

For many years, he worked as a researcher for Britain's curator of oddities Jeremy Beadle, helping him to compile the world's largest database of anniversaries. They also worked on a number of television and radio projects, although none with a sporting theme.

He has worked on most national newspapers at one time or another. For the past 12 years he has written a column on murder in *Master Detective* magazine and for the last two years a trivia column in the *Daily Star*. His idea of fun is getting quizzical with a bunch of strangers in a pub.

FIRST

REFERENCE TO THE SPORT
France. 12th century

Like many sports, the origins of tennis are obscure, with many theories posited. Sporting historians believe the game originated in France and Italy and was played by monks in cloistered monasteries. The monks struck the ball with the palm of their hand giving rise to the name "jeu de paume" ("game of the palm").

FIRST

REFERENCE TO INDOOR COURTS
FRANCE. 13TH CENTURY

King Louis X of France was an enthusiastic practitioner of "jeu de paume" but did not like having to play outside, especially on cold winter days, so he had indoor courts built in Paris.

ONLY

KING TO DIE AFTER PLAYING TENNIS
Louis X of France, Vincennes, Val-de-Marne, France.
Saturday, 5 June 1316

Louis X came to the throne of France on 29 November 1314 following the death of King Philip the Fair. A keen tennis player, he arranged for the first indoor courts to be built. On 5 June 1316, he played a fast game of tennis at Château de Vincennes, Val-de-Marne and downed a large amount of cold wine. He then died of either pleurisy or pneumonia, although there are suspicions of poison.

FIRST

REFERENCE TO A LADY PLAYER

LADY MARGOT, FRANCE. 1427

Lady Margot was an early player of "jeu de paume" and is mentioned in records in 1427. It was said that she could beat most male players (see 1888, 1973).

FIRST

REFERENCE TO A SERVE

HAMPTON COURT PALACE, HAMPTON COURT WAY, EAST MOLESEY KT8 9AU, SURREY. 1531

King Henry VIII was a keen player of real tennis and had courts built at Hampton Court Palace but as the years went by, he became too fat to bend down to pick up the ball. The accounts for Hampton Court in 1531 reveal an entry for five shillings for "one that served on the King's side at Tennes".

FIRST

KNOWN TENNIS BOOK

Trattato del Giuoco della Palla, Venice, Italy. 1555

The first known book about tennis, *Trattato del Giuoco*, was written by an Italian priest, Antonio Scaino da Salothe, and published at Venice in 1555. In the book he writes about racquets, then known as battoirs, which were arranged to suit the individual players and came in various shapes and sizes.

FIRST

REFERENCE TO A FINE
FOR BAD LANGUAGE

France. 1599

Hundreds of years before Superbrat John McEnroe upset umpires with his petulance, the French authorities instigated a fine of five sous for swearing on court.

FIRST

TENNIS BAN

FIRST

MENTION OF TENNIS IN AMERICA

New Netherlands, America. Friday, 30 September 1659

In 1659, Peter Stuyvesant, the last Dutch director-general of the colony of New Netherlands (1647–1664), signed a proclamation that banned the playing of tennis during time set aside for church services. Tennis had become so popular that church congregations had sunk.

ONLY

HEIR TO A THRONE KILLED BY A TENNIS BALL

FREDERICK LOUIS, PRINCE OF WALES, LEICESTER HOUSE, LEICESTER
SQUARE, MIDDLESEX, ENGLAND. WEDNESDAY, 20 MARCH 1751

The unloved and unlovely Frederick Louis, Prince of Wales, died aged
44 leaving his son George – later Mad King George III – as heir to the
throne. Frederick disliked and was disliked by his own father George
II whom he continually pestered for money. The prince was a keen
cricketer, captaining sides for Surrey and London. An abscess in his lung,
burst by a blow from a real tennis ball, is said to have brought about his
death. A rhyme of the time summed up the public feeling:

"Here lies poor Fred who was alive and is dead,

Had it been his father I had much rather,

Had it been his sister nobody would have missed her,

Had it been his brother, still better than another,

Had it been the whole generation, so much better for the nation,

But since it is Fred who was alive and is dead,

There is no more to be said!"

FIRST

LAWN TENNIS CLUB

LEAMINGTON LAWN TENNIS CLUB, MANOR
HOUSE HOTEL, AVENUE ROAD, LEAMINGTON SPA,
WARWICKSHIRE CV31 3NJ ENGLAND. 1872

The first tennis club was founded by Major Harry Gem, his Spanish
friend Augurio Perera, Doctor Arthur Wellesley Tomkins and Doctor
Frederic Haynes. Gem and Perera had been enthusiastic rackets players
and devised a variation called pelota in a nod to Perera's origins, which
became "lawn rackets". The winner was the first player to score 15 points.
In 1872, Gem and Perera joined forces with two young doctors from the
Warneford Hospital to form a club in the grounds of the Manor House
Hotel, Leamington Spa. The club is no longer in existence.

FIRST
LAWN TENNIS PATENT
**SPHAIRISTIKE, MAJOR WALTER CLOPTON WINGFIELD, ENGLAND.
MONDAY, 23 FEBRUARY 1874**

The first tennis patent was awarded to Major Walter Clopton Wingfield (retired) of Belgrave Road, Pimlico, Middlesex, for a "New and Improved Court for Playing the Ancient Game of Tennis". In March, he publicised the game as "Sphairistike" (from the Greek word for ball games), offering the term "lawn tennis" as an explanation. Wingfield sold Sphairistike sets for five guineas – the box included two net posts, a net, rackets, and India rubber balls, plus instructions about how to lay out the court and play the game. Two brothers, Clarence and Joseph Clark, took one of Wingfield's boxes to America, leading to **the first lawn tennis tournament in USA** later that year.

FIRST
US LAWN TENNIS CLUB
**Staten Island Cricket and Baseball Club, Camp Washington, Staten
Island, New York, United States of America. Summer 1875**

The Staten Island Cricket and Baseball Club was founded on 22 March 1872. It is believed the first tennis played in America was at this club. Mary Ewing Outerbridge spent the winter of 1873 in Bermuda where she saw tennis played by the British Army officers stationed there. When she returned to America aboard SS *Canima* on 2 February 1874, she brought a tennis set with her. The directors of the Staten Island Cricket Club gave permission for a net to be erected and soon tennis became very popular with members. **The first American National tournament** was played on 1 September 1880 at the Staten Island Cricket and Baseball Club. Twenty-three men entered the competition, which was won by an Englishman named Otway Woodhouse who received a silver cup worth about $100. It was inscribed "The Champion Lawn Tennis Player of America". In 1906, the name of the club was changed to the Staten Island Cricket and Tennis Club, but changed again in 1931 to the Staten Island Cricket Club.

FIRST

WIMBLEDON
CHAMPIONSHIPS

FIRST

RULES OF TENNIS

FIRST

TENNIS TOURNAMENT
OPEN TO ALL-COMERS

FIRST

WINNER OF THE ALL-COMERS'
GENTLEMEN'S SINGLES TOURNAMENT

All England Croquet and Lawn Tennis Club, The Championships, Worple Road, Wimbledon, Surrey SW, England. Monday, 9 July – Thursday, 19 July 1877

The All England Croquet Club was founded on 23 July 1868 in the offices of *The Field* magazine at 346 Strand in central London, with the editor John H. Walsh being the first chairman. On 24 September 1869, the committee agreed to rent from Alfred Dixon a four-acre site – in what is now Nursery Road, Wimbledon – between Worple Road and the London and South Western Railway. The rent would cost £50, rising to £75 in the second year and £100 in the third. An annual subscription for a lady or gentleman cost a guinea while £1 11s 6d would get a subscription for a couple. A lifetime subscription would be ten guineas for an individual or 15 guineas for a married couple.

A pavilion was built in 1870 and the first croquet tournament was held that year, in June. On 25 February 1875, one of the croquet lawns was set aside for tennis and badminton. On 24 June 1875, the MCC's Laws of Lawn Tennis were officially adopted, although with some modifications – the scoring would be 15, 30, 40, deuce, advantage and only the serving player could add to his score. On 14 April 1877, the club's name was changed to the All England Croquet and Lawn Tennis Club. On 2 June of the same year, the committee approved John Walsh's motion (which was seconded by B. C. Evelegh) "that a public meeting be held on July 10th and following days to compete for The Championships in lawn tennis and that a sub-committee composed of Messrs J. Marshall, H. Jones and C. G. Heathcote be appointed to draw up rules for its management". A week later, The *Field* published a slightly amended advertisement for the competition: "All England Croquet And Lawn Tennis Club, Wimbledon, propose to hold a lawn tennis meeting, open to all amateurs, on Monday, July 9th and following days. Entrance fee £1 1s 0d. Two prizes will be given – one gold champion prize to the winner and one silver to the second player."

Walsh had donated a pony roller for the lawns in return for his daughter being elected to membership of the club, but by 1877, it had broken and so Walsh had come up with the idea of holding the tennis tournament to raise funds to repair it. Julian Marshall, Henry Jones and Charles Gilbert Heathcote decided to adopt the Real Tennis rule that there would be sudden death at five games all and at the end of each set the players changed ends. The net was five feet high at the posts dropping to three feet three inches at the centre.

And so, in the same year that the first cricket Test match was played, the Wimbledon Championships began. The tournament commenced on the second Monday in July with just one competition – the Gentlemen's Singles and there were twenty-two participants each paying a guinea entry fee. Dr Henry Jones, 46, was the tournament referee and even built a bathroom which he charged patrons to use. No one had figured out how to arrange a tournament with 22 players so there were 11 players in the second round and three semi-finalists. To resolve the problem, William C. Marshall was given a bye into the final. Despite it being held in July, the weather for the final was poor.

After the semi-finals on Thursday, 12 July, the tournament was postponed on 13 and 14 July so that crowds could go to watch the Eton v Harrow cricket match at Lord's and return for the final the following Monday, 16 July. However, the Monday was a washout and the game was postponed until the following Thursday. W. Spencer Gore, a 27-year-old surveyor, an Old Harrovian and a keen cricketer, won the first championships and with it a prize of 12 guineas and a silver cup worth 25 guineas. In a match, delayed an hour by rain, Gore beat Cambridge real tennis Blue William C. Marshall 6-1, 6-2, 6-4 in just 48 minutes.

The following year, Gore lost 5-7, 1-6, 7-9 to Frank Hadow in the Challenge Round – the final match contested by the reigning champion and the winner of the all-comers' tournament, until 1922 – and never went back to Wimbledon. He was to write, "That anyone who has really played well at cricket, tennis or even rackets, will ever give his attention seriously to lawn tennis beyond showing himself to be a promising player, is extremely doubtful, for in all probability the monotony of the game as compared with others would choke him off before he had time to excel in it."

DID YOU KNOW?

The All England Lawn Tennis and Croquet Club's colours – introduced in 1909 – are dark green and purple, although no one seems to know why.

ONLY

GRAND SLAM
TOURNAMENT
PLAYED ON GRASS

THE CHAMPIONSHIPS, WORPLE ROAD, WIMBLEDON, SURREY

SW, ENGLAND. 1877–1921; THE CHAMPIONSHIPS, CHURCH
ROAD, WIMBLEDON, SURREY SW, ENGLAND. 1922–1965; THE
CHAMPIONSHIPS, CHURCH ROAD, WIMBLEDON, LONDON SW19
5AE, ENGLAND. 1965–PRESENT DAY

Of the four Grand Slam tournaments, Wimbledon is the only one played
on a natural surface. The Australian Open was played on grass until 1988
before moving to Rebound Ace and then Plexicushion. The French Open
is **the only Grand Slam tournament to use clay courts**. The US Open is
the only major to have been played on three surfaces; it was played on
grass from its inception until 1974, clay from 1975 until 1977 and hard
courts since it moved from the West Side Tennis Club to the United
States National Tennis Center in 1978.

DID YOU KNOW?

In 1913, as part of their violent campaign to get votes for women,
suffragettes tried to burn down the Centre Court stand at Worple
Road, Wimbledon.

FIRST

FRENCH LAWN TENNIS CLUB

Decimal Lawn Tennis and Boating Society, Neuilly-sur-Seine, France. 1877

The first French lawn tennis club was founded in the same year as the
first Wimbledon Championships. The club, unlike the tournament, has
not survived. It is certain that tennis had been played in France before
the club was formed. Indeed, French people were banned from joining
the Decimal and it closed in 1895.

FIRST

CLUB IN AUSTRALIA

ASSOCIATION GROUND LAWN TENNIS CLUB, SYDNEY, NEW SOUTH
WALES, AUSTRALIA. 1878

Lawn tennis was first played on asphalt at Warehouseman's Cricket
Ground on St Kilda Road in Melbourne. Such was the popularity that a
grass court was added in 1879. The first tennis club in Australia was the
Association Ground Lawn Tennis Club founded in Sydney, New South
Wales in 1878.

FIRST

PLAYER TO LOB THE BALL

ONLY

WIMBLEDON CHAMPION TO NOT HAVE LOST A SINGLES SET

ONLY

WIMBLEDON CHAMPION TO OWN A COFFEE PLANTATION

**FRANK HADOW, GENTLEMEN'S SINGLES, THE
CHAMPIONSHIPS, WORPLE ROAD, WIMBLEDON,
SURREY SW, ENGLAND. SATURDAY, 20 JULY 1878**

Frank Hadow was born on 2 January 1855 at Regent's Park and was
educated at Harrow. In the summer of 1878, he was on holiday from
the coffee plantation that he owned in Ceylon when he decided to enter

the Gentlemen's Singles competition at Wimbledon. He got through to the All-Comers' final without losing a set and proceeded to beat Robert Erskine 6-4, 6-4, 6-4. Hadow was the first player to win games by lobbing the ball. In the Challenge Round, he beat the defending champion Spencer Gore 7-5, 6-1, 9-7 to take the title, but that was his only appearance at The Championships. When asked if he would defend his title, Hadow is said to have replied, "No sir. It's a sissy's game played with a soft ball." He died on 29 June 1946 at Bridgwater, Somerset.

FIRST

SCOTTISH LAWN
TENNIS CHAMPIONSHIPS

SCOTTISH CHAMPIONSHIPS, DYVOURS CLUB, RAEBURN PLACE, EDINBURGH, SCOTLAND.
MONDAY, 12 – MONDAY, 19 AUGUST 1878

The Scottish Championships were first held in August 1878 and, after 106 competitions, last held in 1994. From its inauguration, the tournament was held in Edinburgh at the Dyvours Club before moving in 1893 to St Andrews, the home of golf. The first six men's finals were played indoors at Dyvours in "a pavilion of metal construction" known as "the Tin Temple" which "housed two courts, two cramped dressing rooms and a gallery with six rows of seats". **The first Men's Singles winner** was James Patten MacDougall although who he beat and by what score is lost in the mists of time. In 1879, the second tournament was won by Leslie Balfour-Melville, who then lost the 1880 final to James Patten MacDougall. **The first foreign winner** was Anthony Wilding from New Zealand on 13 August 1904. He beat Charles Glenny 6-1, 6-1, 6-2. Donald MacPhail won both the last tournament before the Second World War and the first one (20 July 1946) after the cessation of hostilities. **The first Women's Singles** was held in 1886 and won by Mabel Boulton who beat Julia MacKenzie 3-6, 6-0, 6-2, 4-6, 6-2.

In the Open Era, Britain's Jeremy Bates won the Men's Singles twice (1980 and 1985). In 1989, John McEnroe beat Jimmy Connors 7-6, 7-6. **The last winner of the Men's Singles** was Briton Ken Wood in July 1994 and he beat fellow Briton Malcolm Watt 7-6, 6-2. **The last winner of the Women's Singles** was Heather Lockhart in July 1994 and she beat Alison Reid 6-0, 4-6, 6-4. On 7 August 1994, another Scottish tennis tournament came to an end. The **last finals of the Scottish Hard Court Tennis Championships** were held. The first competition was held from 20 to 25 August 1923 at the St Andrews Lawn Tennis Club, Kinburn Park St Andrews, Fife on clay courts. It stayed there until 1981 when it moved to Fort Hill Tennis Club, Broughty Ferry, Dundee until its end. Ken Wood, 24, added to his trophy tally by beating defending champion Jason Barnett 2-6, 7-6, 6-4. Nineteen-year-old Aberdonian Barnett, a clay-court specialist, was the firm favourite and when he went into a 6-2, 4-2 lead, it looked as though he was set to add the hard-court crown to the indoor title he had won in February, but Wood was determined and he fought back to take the match and championship. In 1992, his sister Allison Wood won the Women's Singles. In 1983, Alison Reid won the title and in **the last Women's Singles final** Reid beat 26-year-old Wood 6-1, 6-2.

FIRST

IRISH LAWN
TENNIS CHAMPIONSHIPS

FIRST

WOMAN TENNIS CHAMPION

Irish Lawn Tennis Championships, Pembroke Place, Dublin, Ireland.
Monday, 2 June – Tuesday, 10 June 1879

Two years after Wimbledon, the first Irish Lawn Tennis Championships (later the Irish Open) were held in Dublin. The first competition was held in Pembroke Place, Dublin and the men's title won by Vere St

Leger Goold, the only Irishman to reach a Wimbledon final. The Championships had the distinction of being the first event to feature men's and women's singles and doubles tournaments as well as a mixed doubles competition. The first woman to win a championship was May Langrishe, who triumphed in a field of seven. She beat Miss D. Meldon 6-2, 0-6, 8-6 in the final when she was just 14 years, 161 days old. The winners of the first Men's Doubles were J. Elliot and H. Kellie but no record exists of their opponents or winning margin. The inaugural Mixed Doubles was won by J. Elliot and Miss Costello. The first Women's Doubles were not held until 1884 when Beatrice Langrishe beat her sister, May.

Before the International Lawn Tennis Federation was founded in 1913, the Irish competition was regarded as one of the big four, along with Wimbledon, the US National Championships and the Northern Championships. In 1880, the competition moved to Wilton Place where it stayed till 1902. In 1903, the tournament moved again, this time to Fitzwilliam Square. The tournament changed its name to the Irish Open in 1972 and again it moved location to Appian Way, Dublin, where it stayed until it ended in 1979 for the men and in 1983 for the ladies.

For the first two tournaments, the players competed on hard courts before playing on grass from 1881 until 1939. From 1946 until 1965 it was played on clay and then grass again from 1966 until 1979 (1983). The last Irishman to win the competition was 6ft 7in George Lyttleton Rogers in 1937.

━━•◆•──

FIRST

WIMBLEDON WINNER
TO RETAIN HIS TITLE

ONLY

CLERGYMAN TO WIN
WIMBLEDON GENTLEMEN'S
ALL-COMERS' SINGLES CHAMPIONSHIPS

ONLY

IRISHMAN TO REACH WIMBLEDON
GENTLEMEN'S ALL-COMERS' SINGLES FINAL

**REVEREND JOHN HARTLEY, GENTLEMEN'S ALL-COMERS'
SINGLES, THE CHAMPIONSHIPS, WORPLE ROAD, WIMBLEDON,
SURREY SW, ENGLAND. TUESDAY, 15 JULY 1879;
GENTLEMEN'S ALL-COMERS' SINGLES, THE CHAMPIONSHIPS,
WORPLE ROAD, WIMBLEDON, SURREY SW, ENGLAND.
WEDNESDAY, 15 JULY 1880**

Born at Tong, Shropshire, on 9 January 1849, John Thorneycroft Hartley
was the grandson of the first Mayor of Wolverhampton, who had made
his fortune with the Shrubbery Ironworks in Horseley Fields. Hartley
went to Harrow and then Oxford, where he won the university Rackets
and Real Tennis Championship. He took holy orders and was appointed
vicar of Burneston, Bedale in North Yorkshire. He began courting Alice
Margaret Lascelles, the granddaughter of the 3rd Earl of Harwood. To
see her, he would ride to a river and swim across it before she collected
him in a carriage.

In 1879 and 1880, Hartley won the third and fourth All England
Lawn Tennis Championships and in 1881 he was the runner-up. At the
1879 tournament, when Hartley was 30 years old, all 45 competitors were
British and 36 of them had never taken part in Wimbledon before. In
the first round, Hartley saw off Charles Cole 6-0, 6-0, 6-3. In the second
round, his opponent was Scotsman Lestocq Erskine, who had played at
the first Wimbledon two years earlier and who took Hartley to five sets.
The clergyman finally won 6-4, 6-5, 5-6, 0-6, 6-5. His next opponent

was William Marshall in the third round and Hartley won 6-1, 6-3, 4-6, 6-1. His quarter-final on Saturday, 12 July 1879 was against barrister Charles Gilbert Heathcote, one of the founders of the All England Club who had played in the first Wimbledon Championships in 1877. After he had seen off Heathcote 6-4, 6-3, 6-3, Hartley caught the train back up to Yorkshire where he took services the next day. Hartley had not expected to get very far in the tournament and so had not arranged cover for his clerical duties. "I had to come home on Saturday, breakfast very early on Monday morning, drive ten miles to a station, get to London at two and get to Wimbledon just in time to play – rather tired by my journey and in want of a meal," he recalled. "I nearly lost that game, the semi-final against Parr, but fortunately it came on to rain. We stopped, I got some tea, felt much refreshed and finished off all right."

It was the only time Cecil Parr entered Wimbledon and he took the first set 6-2, but Hartley regained his form and won the next three sets comprehensively 6-0, 6-1, 6-1. The next day, Hartley was up against Irishman "Mr St Leger" (later revealed to be Vere St Leger Gould, see 1907) who had had a bye in his semi-final. Hartley won the All-Comers' final 6-2, 6-4, 6-3 before 1,100 spectators and received a walkover to take the title because the previous year's winner Frank Hadow did not return to contest the Challenge Round. A year later, Hartley became the first champion to retain his title. As the holder, he did not have to trouble himself with actually winning through to the final, only with playing the Challenge Round. He beat H. F. Lawford 6-3, 6-2, 2-6, 6-3 before 1,300 spectators. Herbert Lawford, 29, had a reputation for a fearsome, topspin forehand but he was not able to bring it to bear against Hartley. For this match, the height of the net was reduced from 4ft 9in at the posts to 4ft.

As reigning champion, Hartley also had a free pass into the 1881 final but this time he lost 6-0, 6-1, 6-1 in just 37 minutes to Willie Renshaw, one of twins, who would go on to become **the first player to win the trophy for six consecutive years**. This was the shortest final on record and it was said that Hartley was suffering from an attack of "English cholera". Hartley did not compete in 1882 and in 1883 he lost in the second round to Herbert Wilberforce 6-4, 5-6, 2-6, 4-6 after which he retired from competitive tennis and returned to tend his flock. He was appointed Rural Dean of East Catterick in 1891 and Honorary Canon of Ripon in 1906. He died at Knaresborough on 21 August 1935, aged 86.

DID YOU KNOW?

In 1926, at the Golden Jubilee championships, HM Queen Mary presented the 34 surviving champions – including John Hartley – with a silver medal.

FIRST
TOURNAMENT IN AUSTRALIA
Melbourne, Victoria, Australia. 1880

The first tennis tournament in Australia was the Victorian Championships, held in Melbourne in 1880. The winner was A.F. Robinson.

FIRST
RECORDED DEATH ON A TENNIS COURT
COLONEL OSBORNE, HYDE PARK TENNIS CLUB, HYDE PARK, LONDON W. 1880S

The death of Colonel Osborne who had been playing at the Hyde Park Tennis Club was the first death recorded on a tennis court.

DID YOU KNOW?

Members of The All England Lawn Tennis and Croquet Club can use the courts at Wimbledon all year round except for the Centre and No 1 courts – and while The Championships are being played.

FIRST

UNITED STATES
NATIONAL CHAMPIONSHIPS

FIRST

WINNER OF THE UNITED STATES
NATIONAL CHAMPIONSHIPS MEN'S SINGLES

FIRST

WINNERS OF THE
UNITED STATES NATIONAL CHAMPIONSHIPS

MEN'S DOUBLES

**United States National Championships, Newport
Casino, 186-202 Bellevue Avenue, Newport, Rhode
Island 02840 United States of America. Wednesday,
31 August – Saturday, 3 September 1881**

The United States National Lawn Tennis Association (USNLTA) was founded on 21 May 1881 in Room F at the Fifth Avenue Hotel, New York and comprised 34 clubs. The first president was Robert Shaw Oliver of the Albany Tennis Club. That same year, on 31 August, the USNLTA held its first National Championships, which would evolve into the US Open. There were two competitions in the first tournament which was held at Newport Casino – Men's Singles and Men's Doubles. The first winner of the Men's Singles title was Dick Sears, a 19-year-old student at Harvard, who had only begun playing tennis two years earlier. He became **the first player to win the singles competition seven years in a row**. In his first three championships, Sears did not lose a single set. As with Wimbledon, however, the champion only had to beat the winner of the All-Comers' competition to retain their title. He was also **the first**

player to win the doubles title six times in a row, from 1882 to 1887 and then retired from competitive tennis. Sears was the first US No 1 in the USNLTA rankings, when they started in 1885 and held the ranking in 1886 and 1887.

Apart from the final, each match was decided on the best of three sets and the first to six games won. Only members of United States National Lawn Tennis Association were allowed to enter so all 24 entrants were American. In the first round Sears beat H.W. Powell 6-0, 6-2. In the second round he beat a player known only as Anderson 6-1, 6-2. He despatched his quarter-final opponent C. A. Nightingale 6-3, 6-5 and then beat Edward Gray in the semi-final 6-3, 6-0. In the final he beat William Glyn 6-0, 6-3, 6-2. Glyn was actually English, being born at Wycliffe, County Durham, but played for the Staten Island Cricket and B. B. Club. The Doubles Championship was won by Clarence Clark and Frederick Winslow Taylor who beat Arthur Newbold and Alexander Van Rensselaer 6-5, 6-4, 6-5. The Newport Casino staged the US National Championships until 1914.

FIRST

SCOTTISH LAWN TENNIS CLUB

PERTH LAWN TENNIS CLUB, BALHOUSIE STREET, PERTH, SCOTLAND. 1881

The Perth Lawn Tennis Club was the first to be founded in Scotland. Members of the Perth Curling Club secured some ground in Balhousie Street where the original club was established.

FIRST

FLOODLIT LAWN TENNIS COURT

CHELTENHAM, GLOUCESTERSHIRE, ENGLAND. 1881

The first game to be lit by floodlights took place in Cheltenham.

TENNIS TALK

"They've lost my page. Somebody ripped it out. But I'm the main sponsor for the tour! I'm the guy who paid the most fines, so they should give me respect. There should be a page saying 'This is the guy who paid the most fines'."

Goran Ivanišević on being left
out of the ATP player's guide, 2004

FIRST
OVERSEAS PLAYERS IN THE GENTLEMEN'S SINGLES TOURNAMENT

FIRST
WINNERS OF THE GENTLEMEN'S DOUBLES TOURNAMENT

FIRST
TWINS TO WIN THE GENTLEMEN'S DOUBLES TOURNAMENT

FIRST
WINNERS OF THE LADIES' SINGLES TOURNAMENT

FIRST
LADIES' SINGLES FINAL BETWEEN TWO SISTERS

The Championships, All England Lawn Tennis Club, Worple Road, Wimbledon, Surrey SW, England. Saturday, 5 – Saturday, 19 July 1884

The 1884 Wimbledon Championships was memorable for a number of reasons. James Dwight, Arthur Rives and Dick Sears from the United States became the first foreign competitors in the Gentlemen's Singles tournament.

Dwight, known as "the founding father of American tennis", had been one of the founders of the United States National Lawn Tennis Association in 1881 and was its president for 21 years. Like Dwight Davis, he attended Harvard.

At Wimbledon in 1884, he was knocked out in five sets in the second round by the Briton Herbert Chipp. Arthur Rives had himself been knocked out by Chipp in the first round 6-1, 6-2, 6-1. Dick Sears did not play, giving a walkover to his opponent Charles Grinstead.

The first Ladies' Singles tournament was also held that year. There were 13 competitors including the Watson sisters Maud and Lilian, the Harrow, Middlesex-born daughters of a vicar, who received a bye in the first round. Lilian beat Mrs G.J. Cooper in the quarter-finals 7-5, 5-7, 6-3 and then faced M. Leslie, who had received a bye in the quarter-finals. Lilian won the semi-final easily, 6-4, 6-1 and faced baby sister Maud in the final. In the first round, Maud had beaten Mrs A. Tyrwhitt Drake 6-0, 6-2, before overcoming B.E. Williams in the quarter-final 7-5, 6-0. In the semi-final, she beat Blanche Bingley 3-6, 6-4, 6-2. Maud beat Lilian 6-8, 6-3, 6-3 to become Wimbledon's first ladies' champion. The first prize for the ladies' title was 20 guineas while the runner-up received ten guineas. From 1879 until 1883, the Gentlemen's Doubles had been hosted by the Oxford University Club and in 1884 it came under the Wimbledon umbrella for the first time. Twenty competitors entered the first tournament, including the Renshaw twins Willie and Ernest. In the first round they saw off a pair of Herberts – Lawford and Wilberforce – 6-3, 6-3, 4-6, 6-2. In the quarter-finals they played George Butterworth and Wilfred Milne and won in five sets 4-6, 3-6, 7-5, 6-2, 6-2. In the semi-finals they came up against the American tourists James Dwight and Richard Sears winning in straight sets 6-0, 6-1, 6-2. In the final the Renshaws defeated Ernest Lewis and Teddy Williams 6-3, 6-1, 1-6, 6-4. They retained their title in 1885 and 1886 and again won the title in 1888 and 1889. In 1887 they did not defend their title because, ironically, Willie was suffering from a severe case of tennis elbow.

Neither Renshaw twin lived to see old age and neither married. They were born on 3 January 1861 at Brandon Parade, Leamington, Warwickshire. Legend has it they learned to play tennis on the court established by Major Harry Gem and his Spanish friend Augurio Perera (see 1872). In 1879, they entered The Championships at Wimbledon but were too scared to play, so just stayed to watch and learn. They made their debut at Wimbledon in 1880. They were the first to introduce an overarm serve. Their last appearance was in 1893 when – there being no seeds – they were drawn against each other in the first round. Willie withdrew in favour of Ernest but he was knocked out in the next round. Ernest died on 2 September 1899 at The Grange, Waltham St Lawrence, near Twyford, Berkshire. He was 38 and mystery surrounds his. death He died from the effects of spirit of carbolic acid but it is unknown whether he swallowed it accidentally or intended to commit suicide. He left £49,938 14s 9d (£6,315,000 at 2020 values).

Willie died on 12 August 1904 at Swanage, Dorset after suffering epileptic seizures. He was 43. He left £61,604 6s (£7,345,000 at 2020 values). Their family donated the Renshaw Cup to the All England Club and for many years it was given to the winner of the Gentlemen's Singles. They were both inducted into the International Tennis Hall of Fame in 1983.

DID YOU KNOW?

Blanche Bingley played in 13 Ladies' Singles finals at Wimbledon. She took the title in 1886, 1889, 1894, 1897, 1899 and 1900. She lost in 1885, 1887, 1888, 1891, 1892, 1893 and 1901. She also won the Irish championships on three occasions (1888, 1894 and 1897); the German Championship at Hamburg twice (1897 and 1900); and the South of England Championships at

Eastbourne 11 times between 1885 and 1905. On 13 July 1887, a week after the Wimbledon final, she married Commander George Whiteside Hillyard in Greenford, Middlesex. In 1907, he became secretary of the All England Lawn Tennis Club and director of The Championships at Wimbledon, two posts he held until 1925. He died at Bramfold, Pulborough, on 24 March 1943. She died in London on 6 August 1946. She was inducted into the International Tennis Hall of Fame in 2013.

FIRST
LAWN TENNIS AT QUEEN'S CLUB
QUEEN'S CLUB, PALLISER ROAD, HAMMERSMITH, LONDON W14 9EQ, ENGLAND. FRIDAY, 1 JULY 1887

The Queen's Club has played host to many sports since it was founded on 19 August 1886 by Evan Charteris, George Francis and Algernon Grosvener. It was the world's second multi-sport complex (after the Prince's Club) and became the sole one when the Prince's Club moved to Knightsbridge. The Queen in the name is Queen Victoria, who was the first patron. The first tennis courts were opened on 19 May 1887 and the first match was held just under six weeks later when Cambridge met Oxford. It was not until January the following year that the club had its first buildings, designed incidentally by William C. Marshall, the runner-up in the first Wimbledon final in 1877. Members could participate in tennis, real tennis, Eton Fives, rackets, football, rugby and athletics. It was the venue for sporting events between Cambridge and Oxford universities from 1888 to 1928. It was used for the 1908 Olympics and on 18 March 1895 England drew 1-1 with Wales in the only football international held there.

DID YOU KNOW?
Since May 2007, Queen's Club has been owned by its members. If you are aged over 28 and want to join to play off-peak, there is an eight-year waiting list and if you do get accepted you have to buy a redeemable share. The current (2020) price per share is £15,000.

FIRST

WINNER OF UNITED STATES NATIONAL CHAMPIONSHIPS WOMEN'S SINGLES

ELLEN HANSELL, WOMEN'S SINGLES, UNITED STATES NATIONAL CHAMPIONSHIPS, PHILADELPHIA CRICKET CLUB, WISSAHICKON INN, PHILADELPHIA, PENNSYLVANIA 19128, UNITED STATES OF AMERICA. WEDNESDAY, 5 OCTOBER 1887

Six years after the men began playing their competition, the first Women's Singles competition was held. It took place almost a month after the men had finished and in a different location – the outdoor grass courts of the Philadelphia Cricket Club. There were seven competitors, all local (one dropped out after a family bereavement). One of them was 17-year-old Ellen Hansell who had been anaemic as a child and had taken up tennis on her doctor's advice. When she was 16, she joined the Belmont Club in Philadelphia at an annual subscription of $10. To save money, she walked the mile and a half to the club rather than pay five cents for a ride. Hansell entered the first competition and used a squared-off racquet and served sidearm, wearing a full over-draped skirt with long sleeves and red hat when she played. She said, "We did now and then grip our over-draped voluminous skirts with our left hand to give us a bit more limb freedom when dashing to make a swift, snappy stroke." She beat Laura Knight 6-1, 6-0 in a one-sided final. One report stated that she "employed sidearm serves, sliced ground strokes and never, but never went to the net". The following year, Hansell did not succeed in defending her title, losing to Bertha Townsend, 6-3, 6-5 in the challenge match. Hansell retired from competitive tennis in 1890, deciding instead to concentrate on looking after her husband, Taylor Allerdice, and their six children. Hansell died on 11 May 1937 and was inducted into the International Tennis Hall of Fame in 1965.

DID YOU KNOW?

The two women's competitions in 1887 and 1888 were not official and were only recognised retroactively in 1889 on the formation of the United States National Ladies Tennis Association.

FIRST

"BATTLE OF THE SEXES"

Ernest Renshaw v Charlotte Dod, Exmouth Ground, Exmouth, Devon, England. Monday, 13 August 1888

Ernest Renshaw (see 1884), the 27-year-old winner of the Gentleman's Singles in 1888, took on Charlotte Dod, the Ladies' champion in front of a large crowd, who paid a shilling each to watch the contest. To give 17-year-old Dod a chance, Renshaw agreed to a handicap – a 30-0 lead in each game. Dod took a 4-0 lead and then "Renshaw perceived he had no ordinary lady opponent, and from that moment every stroke was keenly contested, both players doing their utmost to ensure victory". Dod won the first set 6-2. At one stage in the second set, Renshaw led by five games to three before Dod rallied and made it five all. Renshaw's strength allowed him to take the match by winning the last two sets 7-5. Both players had won 16 games but Renshaw had taken 95 points to Dod's 52. A local report stated, "Miss Dod surprised the spectators by the brilliancy of her play, several times going to the net to score by volleys. She played so well that Renshaw had to run about as much as against a first-rate player of his own sex. The lady could not, of course, stand the strain so well as her opponent, and palpably tired towards the end."

FIRST

PLAYER TO WIN THE
UNITED STATES NATIONAL CHAMPIONSHIPS
WOMEN'S SINGLES IN
CONSECUTIVE YEARS

Bertha Townsend, Women's Singles, United States National Championships, Philadelphia Cricket Club, Wissahickon Inn, Philadelphia, Pennsylvania 19128, United States of America. Friday, 15 June 1888; Women's Singles, United States National Championships, Philadelphia Cricket Club, Wissahickon Inn, Philadelphia, Pennsylvania 19128, United States of America. Saturday, 15 June 1889

Bertha Louise Townsend was born on 7 March 1869 and beat Marion Wright 6-2, 6-2 in the second All-Comers' final of the US Women's National Singles tennis championship in 1888. She then beat defending champion Ellen Hansell (see 1887) 6-3, 6-5 in the Challenge Round. The following year, she faced Lida Voorhees in the Challenge Round and retained her title, winning 7-5, 6-2. She failed to make it a hat-trick of victories, losing to Ellen Roosevelt 6-2, 6-2 in front of a crowd of almost 2,000. Roosevelt had beaten Lida Voorhees 6-3, 6-1 in the final of the All-Comers' competition to reach the Challenge Round. Bertha Townsend died aged only 40 on 12 May 1909 and was inducted into the International Tennis Hall of Fame in 1974.

ONLY

IRISHWOMAN TO WIN
WIMBLEDON LADIES' SINGLES FINAL

Lena Rice, Ladies' Singles, The Championships, All England Lawn Tennis Club, Worple Road, Wimbledon, Surrey SW, England. Saturday, 5 July 1890

Helena Bertha Grace Rice, who won Wimbledon in 1890, had a number of things in common with her contemporary Charlotte "Lottie" Dod. Both lost fathers when they were young – Rice was two and Dod eight. Both began playing tennis with elder sisters called Anne (Ann in Dod's case) and neither married. Rice was born at County Tipperary in 1866.

The Rice sisters joined the Cahir Lawn Tennis Club. In May 1889, Helena entered the Irish Championships at Dublin and was defeated in straight sets by Blanche Bingley Hillyard in the semi-finals. She and Hillyard lost in the final of the Ladies' Doubles but Rice won the

Mixed Doubles with Willoughby Hamilton. Later that year, Rice went to Wimbledon for the first time and reached the final, where she played Blanche Bingley Hillyard again. Rice took the first set 6-4 and had three match points at 5-3, 40-15 in the second when Hillyard fought back to win 8-6 and then take the final set 6-4. The 1890 Wimbledon Ladies' competition had the smallest entry for any event at The Championships – just four competitors. Rice beat Mary Steedman 7-5, 6-2 in the "semi-finals" and beat May Jacks 6-4, 6-1 in the final to take the title. There was no challenge final as Hillyard was pregnant. Rice has another claim to fame, as it is believed she created the overhead smash, using it to beat Jacks in the match-winning point. Rice did not return to Wimbledon in 1891 to defend her title and no evidence exists of her playing competitive tennis again. She died on 21 June 1907 – her 41st birthday – from tuberculosis.

——•◆•◆◆•◆•——

FIRST

FRENCH CHAMPIONSHIPS

CHAMPIONNAT DE FRANCE INTERNATIONAL DE TENNIS, CERCLE DES SPORT DE L'ILE PUTEAUX, PARIS, FRANCE. 1891

The first French tennis championship (Championnat de France International de Tennis, now the French Open) was held in 1891 and played on grass. The tournament was only open to French tennis players or members of French clubs – a rule that stayed in place until 1925 when it was opened up to the rest of the world and became the fourth of the majors and a Grand Slam tournament. The first winner, however, was an Englishman, H. Briggs, who was a resident of Paris. He beat the Frenchman P. Baigneres 6-3, 6-2 at the Cercle des Sport de l'Ile Puteaux. The women did not compete until 1897 when four ladies participated. **The first Women's Singles champion** was Adine Masson who beat P. Girod 6-3, 6-1. The Mixed Doubles competition was added in 1902 and the Women's Doubles became an event in 1907. André Vacherot was **the first player to win the title three consecutive times** (1894-1896). He was also the oldest victor at 40 when he won the title in 1901. Paul Aymé was **the first player to win the title four consecutive times** (1897-1900). The winner of the Men's Singles event receives the Coupe des Mousquetaires, named after the Four Musketeers of French tennis: Jean Borotra, Jacques Brugnon, Henri Cochet and René Lacoste.

The first French Open began on 28 May 1925 on the outdoor clay courts at the Stade Français in Paris. **The first Men's Singles winner** was Lacoste, who beat Borotra 7-5, 6-1, 6-4. They then pooled their talents to win **the first Men's Doubles competition**, beating Cochet and Brugnon 7-5, 4-6, 6-3, 2-6, 6-3. Brugnon did win a competition that year when he partnered Suzanne Lenglen to win **the first Mixed Doubles title**, beating Julie Vlasto and Cochet, 6-2, 6-2. Lenglen also won **the first Women's Singles title** by defeating Englishwoman Kitty McKane 6-1, 6-2, and she completed a hat-trick to win all three competitions she entered, taking **the first Ladies Doubles' title** with Vlasto, beating the Englishwomen McKane and Evelyn Colyer 6-1, 9-11, 6-2.

FIRST
OLYMPIC MEN'S SINGLES TENNIS GOLD
FIRST
OLYMPIC MEN'S DOUBLES TENNIS GOLD
John Boland, Great Britain and Ireland, Men's Singles, Athens, Greece. Saturday, 11 April 1896; John Boland, Great Britain and Ireland, and Friedrich "Fritz" Traun, Germany, Men's Doubles, Athens, Greece. Saturday, 11 April 1896

The son of a Dublin baker, John Mary Pius Boland became an orphan at age 12. After a spell at London University, he went up to Christ Church,

Oxford to read law. In 1894, Boland invited a Greek acquaintance, Thrasyvoalos Manos, to speak at the Oxford Union. His guest chose as his subject the revival of the Modern Olympic Games that were due to take place in Athens in April 1896. Boland and Manos became close friends and Boland was invited to spend the Easter holidays of 1896 in Athens.

One night at dinner he got chatting to Dionysios Kasdaglis, a Greek from Alexandria, Egypt. Kasdaglis suggested that Boland enter the Olympic tennis tournament and the next morning Boland enrolled, the day before the competition was due to start. Boland had no sporting equipment with him and played in leather shoes with a heel. To his surprise, he won three games – beating Friedrich "Fritz" Traun of Germany in the first round, Evangelis Rallis of Greece in the second and Konstantinos Paspatis of Greece in the semi-finals. To his greater surprise and dismay, he learned his opponent in the final on 11 April was his new friend, Kasdaglis. Boland considered throwing the game but decided that would be dishonourable. He won gold 6-2, 6-2. Boland had also entered the doubles event with Traun, the German runner whom he had beaten in the first round of the singles. Traun had gone to Athens to take part in the 880m race and then joined the tennis competition for fun. When his original partner fell ill, Traun and Boland joined forces and won the doubles event. They beat Aristidis and Konstantinos Akratopoulos of Greece in the first round, had a bye in the semi-finals, and defeated Kasdaglis and Demetrios Petrokokkinos of Greece in the final, also on 11 April. At the winners' ceremony, Olympic officials prepared to raise the Union and German flags but Boland objected, saying that he was Irish and wanted the tricolour flown. Later that year, Boland graduated and the following year was called to the Bar, although he never practised. In 1900, he was elected Irish Parliamentary Party MP for South Kerry, a seat he held until 1918. From 1926 until 1947, he was General Secretary of the Catholic Truth Society. He died at his home in Westminster, London on St Patrick's Day 1958.

FIRST

DAVIS CUP

**USA V GREAT BRITAIN, LONGWOOD CRICKET CLUB, 564
HAMMOND STREET, CHESTNUT HILL, MASSACHUSETTS
02467, UNITED STATES OF AMERICA. WEDNESDAY, 8 –
FRIDAY, 10 AUGUST 1900**

On 4 February 2004, Mark Zuckerberg took a step towards worldwide
fame when he launched Facebook while at Harvard. In 1900, a fourth-
year student at Harvard, Dwight F. Davis also did something which
had long-lasting implications, when he donated the trophy that would
become synonymous with him.

The first Wimbledon Championships had taken place in 1877 and
four years later the United States National Lawn Tennis Association
(USNLTA) had been formed. James Dwight, the first president of the
USNLTA, envisaged a competition between the best players from both
countries. He attempted to bring the best of Britain's players to America
and sent, unofficially, the best US players to play in Britain. By the
mid-1890s there were tours of Britain and the United States. In 1892,
England and Ireland began competing in a competition that was akin to
the eventual Davis Cup. Three years later, in 1895, England played France
in a national team competition. In 1896, William Larned toured the
British Isles and returned to America with the exciting news that Britain
had agreed to send three players to America to tour in the summer of
1897. It would be the first British tennis team in America. By coincidence,
as Larned was leaving, a tennis tournament was held at Niagara-on-the-
Lake, Ontario. Several of those involved spoke of an international tennis
tournament. Among those attending was Dwight F. Davis and someone
suggested he might "do something for the game … put up some big
prize, or cup". In 1897, three British players arrived to compete in several
US tournaments. They did not perform well but Davis was not deterred
and arranged a tournament at Newcastle in July 1898. However, the tour
was aborted when America could not find any players of a high enough
standard. The following year, a mutual tour to the United States garnered
only one British entrant as many of the players were involved in the
Boer War. In 1900, the first in a competition series between Britain and

America including Dwight Davis was played at the Longwood Cricket Club in Boston, Massachusetts. Davis spent about $1,000 of his own money to order a trophy – a sterling silver punchbowl from Shreve, Crump & Low. They then commissioned a classically styled design from William B. Durgin's of Concord, New Hampshire, crafted by the Englishman Rowland Rhodes. Davis had the cup engraved as the "International Lawn Tennis Challenge Trophy", but it soon took his name. In the same way that England were shocked to lose 1-0 to America in the 1950 World Cup, so the United States surprised the British Isles by winning the first three Davis Cup matches. There was no competition in 1901 but on 6–8 August 1902 the United States, again including Dwight Davis, won the International Lawn Tennis Challenge Trophy by three matches to two at the Crescent Athletic Club at Narrows Avenue and 85th Street, Brooklyn, New York, the site of the Fort Hamilton HS Athletic Field. On 4–8 August 1903 at the Longwood Cricket Club, **Britain won the Davis Cup for the first time** by four matches to one. The trophy was then called the Dwight F. Davis International Challenge Cup. The Americans did not actually win any matches on the turf – they were awarded the match between American captain William Larned and Reggie Doherty because the Englishman could not play because of a strained shoulder.

DID YOU KNOW?

Apart from having a leading tennis tournament named after him, Dwight Filley Davis served as US Secretary of War from October 1925 to 1929 and was appointed Governor-General of the Philippines by President Herbert Hoover, serving from 1929 to 1932 when he resigned because of his wife's poor health. On the tennis court, Davis was a finalist in the All-Comers' Men's Singles at the US Championships in 1898 and 1899. With Holcombe Ward, he won the Men's Doubles title at The Championships for three years in a row from 1899 to 1901. Davis and Ward were also Gentlemen's Doubles runners-up at Wimbledon in 1901. During the First World War, he was awarded the Distinguished Service Cross for "extraordinary heroism in action". A Republican, he died, aged 66, of a heart attack at his home in Washington DC on 28 November 1945. He was buried in Arlington National Cemetery.

FIRST
DAVIS CUP OUTSIDE AMERICA

FIRST
DAVIS CUP TO FEATURE
TEAMS OTHER THAN
BRITAIN AND USA

Dwight F. Davis International Challenge Cup,
Worple Road, Wimbledon, Surrey SW, England.
Monday, 27 June – Tuesday, 5 July 1904

With the British Isles having won the third competition in 1903, they got the chance to host for the first time. It was not only the first Davis Cup not on American soil, it was the first to feature non-Anglosphere teams when France and Belgium entered. The Americans sat out the competition, being unable to muster a team. Beginning on 27 June 1904, the French and Belgians played out five games – four singles matches and one doubles. The Belgians won three matches to two – the French winning the doubles and gaining a victory when Belgian captain Paul de Borman retired hurt although he was 6-4, 5-3 down at the time.

The Belgians went on to meet the British in the finals and were comprehensively beaten five games to love. Gradually, more teams entered the competition – Australasia, Austria (both 1905), Germany (1913), Canada (1914), South Africa (1919), Holland (1920), and so on until most countries that play tennis entered – at the last count more than 140. The Open Era began in 1968 but the Davis Cup did not allow professionals to compete until 1973. In 1989, the tie-break was introduced into Davis Cup competition, and from 2016 it was used in all five sets.

FIRST

AMERICAN WOMAN TO WIN
LADIES' SINGLES AT WIMBLEDON

FIRST

FOREIGN WOMAN TO WIN
LADIES' SINGLES AT WIMBLEDON

**MAY SUTTON, LADIES' SINGLES, THE CHAMPIONSHIPS,
WORPLE ROAD, WIMBLEDON, SURREY SW, ENGLAND.
FRIDAY, 7 JULY 1905**

May Sutton was born at Plymouth on 25 September 1886, the youngest of seven children and daughter of a Royal Navy captain. In 1892, the family emigrated to the United States for her father's health – he suffered from respiratory problems – and they settled on a ranch near Pasadena, California. Sutton won her first tournament when she was 13. In 1904, she competed in the US National Championships and won the singles and doubles titles at the first attempt. The following year, 5ft 4in Sutton became only the second American woman to compete at The Championships (the 1899 US champion, Marion Jones, had reached the quarter-finals on her only appearance at Wimbledon in 1900) and the first American to win the Ladies' Singles title. She is **the only American champion born in Great Britain**. Sutton shocked the staid Wimbledon crowd by exposing both her ankles and her wrists when she played. In her first-round match she beat N. Meyer 6-0, 6-0. Her second-round opponent, also British, was Ellen Stawell-Brown. Sutton won 6-3, 6-1. In the third round she beat Winifred Longhurst 6-3, 6-1. Her quarter-final opponent Ethel Thomson pushed her hard, taking a 5-2 lead in the first set before Sutton won 8-6, 6-1. A 6-4, 6-0 victory over Agatha Morton took Sutton into the All-Comers' final, in which she beat Constance Wilson 6-3, 8-6 on Thursday, 6 July 1905. *The Times* reported that Sutton "kept a good length and seldom allowed her opponent to come up to the net". In the Challenge Round, Sutton faced the defending champion Dorothea Douglass, who had won the title in 1903 and 1904. Douglass won the first game but Sutton rallied and won the next five to take the first set 6-3. Using an excellent forehand, Sutton dominated the rallies from the back of the court, winning the match and the championship 6-4.

The following year, Sutton and Douglass returned to the final, as they did in 1907. In 1906, Douglass won 6-3, 9-7 but in 1907 Sutton won her second and final Ladies' Singles title beating Douglass (by then Mrs Lambert Chambers) 6-1, 6-4, having not dropped a set en route to the final. Molla Mallory, who won the US National Championship eight times, said of Sutton, "Her drive was the fastest and the … most difficult … to handle, because it dove suddenly to the ground and then jumped up unexpectedly with queer curves. When she could keep her drives near the baseline, they either forced me back farther than I had been accustomed to play or compelled me to make errors. She was also strong overhead when she came to the net and altogether had more power and effectiveness than any other woman tennis player of her time."

In 1912, after marrying and raising a family, Sutton went into semi-retirement. She played her last game at Wimbledon in 1929 when she reached the semi-final. In 1928 and 1929, she and her daughter Dorothy Cheney became **the only mother-daughter combination to be seeded at the US Championships**. She was inducted into the International Tennis Hall of Fame in 1956 and died of cancer at Santa Monica, California on 4 October 1975.

DID YOU KNOW?

Ellen Stawell-Brown, who played at The Championships from 1901 until 1905, was the first woman to serve overarm at Wimbledon. Her daughter, Susan Billington, was the last player to serve underarm. She played in the Ladies' and Mixed Doubles from 1946 until 1956. Billington reached the third round in the Ladies' Doubles in 1951, 1955 and 1956. Her grandson (and Stawell-Brown's great-grandson) is Tim Henman.

FIRST
DAVIS CUP TO FEATURE AUSTRALASIA
**DWIGHT F. DAVIS INTERNATIONAL CHALLENGE CUP, QUEEN'S CLUB,
PALLISER ROAD, HAMMERSMITH, LONDON W14 9EQ, ENGLAND.
THURSDAY, 13 – WEDNESDAY, 19 JULY 1905**

A combined Australia and New Zealand under the banner Australasia competed in the Davis Cup for the first time in 1905. Australasia's first opponents were Austria and they easily won five matches to love. The three-man Australasian team comprised Norman Brookes, Anthony Wilding and Alfred Dunlop, the latter two being New Zealanders while Brookes was the sole Australian. The joint venture was not a sign of colonial camaraderie but that Brookes and Wilding, both rich men, were able to afford to travel, spending much time overseas doing nothing but play tennis. Wilding was already based in England, having gone to Cambridge University. In the final against the United States, the Australasians were unable to replicate their form against Austria and lost the competition by five matches to love. The Americans went three games up which meant they had won the right to meet the British Isles in the Challenge Round and the Australasians did not want to complete the dead rubber. The rules meant they had to and Beals C. Wright beat Wilding 6-3, 6-3; William Larned saw off Norman Brookes 14-12, 6-3, 6-0.

FIRST
AUSTRALASIAN CHAMPIONSHIPS

FIRST
COMMERCIALLY SPONSORED GRAND SLAM EVENT

FIRST
GRAND SLAM EVENT TO BE PLAYED INDOORS

AUSTRALASIAN CHAMPIONSHIPS, WAREHOUSEMAN'S CRICKET GROUND, ST KILDA ROAD, MELBOURNE, VICTORIA 3000, AUSTRALIA. TUESDAY, 21 – SATURDAY, 25 NOVEMBER 1905

The first Australian tennis championship began in November 1905 and was played at the Warehouseman's Cricket Ground in Melbourne. There were 17 players in the first singles event, which was won by Australian Rodney Heath, who beat Albert Curtis, 4-6, 6-3, 6-4, 6-4. Known originally as the Australasian Championships, it became the Australian Championships in 1927 and the Australian Open in 1969. It has actually been held across five Australian and two New Zealand cities: Melbourne (55 times), Sydney (17 times), Adelaide (14 times), Brisbane (seven times), Perth (three times), Christchurch (1906) and Hastings (1912). It did not become one of the majors until 1924, when players began to be seeded. In 1972 it was decided that the tournament would find a permanent home in Melbourne as that city attracted the biggest crowds. The competition was played at the Kooyong Lawn Tennis Club from 1972 until it moved to the new Melbourne Park complex in 1988. For many years, only Australian and New Zealand players participated because of the distance involved in travelling Down Under – it could take up to 45 days by boat. Even when the tournament moved into the Open Era it was not until 1982 that many of the best players took part because of the distance, the inconvenience of the dates (usually around Christmas and New Year's Day) and the small prize money. The Australian Open was the first major to have a commercial sponsor. From 1974 until 1984 it was sponsored by Marlboro cigarettes and from 1985 until 1997 by Ford. Until 1988, the competition was played on grass but then they switched to a rubberised hard court known as Rebound Ace, then Plexicushion. Now? Of the four Grand Slam events, the Australian Open is the best attended with 796,435 people attending the 2019 tournament. The Australian Open was also the first Grand Slam tournament to be played indoors during wet weather or extreme hot weather. The Margaret Court Arena was the first to be fitted with a retractable roof. It was followed by the Rod Laver Arena and the Melbourne Arena.

TENNIS TALK

"I love Wimbledon. But why don't they stage it in the summer?"

Vijay Amritraj on a wetter
than usual Championships, 2007

FIRST

FOREIGN WINNER
OF GENTLEMEN'S
ALL-COMERS' SINGLES AT WIMBLEDON

FIRST

LEFT-HANDED WINNER OF
GENTLEMEN'S ALL-COMERS'
SINGLES AT WIMBLEDON

**NORMAN BROOKES, GENTLEMEN'S ALL-COMERS' SINGLES, THE
CHAMPIONSHIPS, WORPLE ROAD, WIMBLEDON, SURREY SW,
ENGLAND. FRIDAY, 5 JULY 1907**

Born on 14 November 1877 in the St Kilda suburb of Melbourne,
Norman Everard Brookes was the son of an English immigrant who got
rich from gold mining. At school, Brookes was good at cricket, Australian
football and tennis. It helped that his family had their own tennis court at
their mansion on Queens Road, Melbourne, where he practised, as well as
at the local Lorne Street courts. His first visit to Wimbledon was in 1905
when he beat Sydney Smith 1-6, 6-4, 6-1, 1-6, 7-5 in the All-Comers'
final. However, he lost to the Reigning Champion Laurence Doherty
8-6, 6-2, 6-4 in the challenge round. Two years later, in 1907, on his
second visit to The Championships, Brookes became the first non-British
player and the first left-hander to win the Gentlemen's Singles title at

Wimbledon after a straight sets victory – 6-4, 6-2, 6-2 – in the final against 39-year-old Arthur Gore, after the reigning champion Laurence Doherty did not defend his title. Brookes also won the Gentlemen's Doubles that year with New Zealander Anthony Wilding. In April the following year, Brookes cancelled his trip to London to defend his title because his father was unwell. William Brookes died in 1910 and Brookes had to devote more time to Australian Paper Mills, the family business. He did not return to Wimbledon until 1914 when, in the second round, Brookes beat Briton L.F. Davin 6-0, 6-0, 6-0. His third-round opponent was Major Ritchie 6-1, 6-0, 6-1. (Major was his first name, not a military rank.) In the fourth round, he beat Briton W. Clements 6-3, 6-0, 6-0, then in the quarter-final he played old rival Arthur Gore and won 7-5, 6-1, 6-2. In the semi-final, he beat the Briton Alfred Beamish 6-0, 6-3, 6-2. His first non-British opponent came in the All-Comers' final when he faced German Otto Froitzheim. Brookes won 6-2, 6-1, 5-7, 4-6, 8-6 and then beat the teetotal, non-smoking reigning champion Anthony Wilding 6-4, 6-4, 7-5 in the Challenge Round to win the Gentlemen's Singles tennis title. Brookes and Wilding also again won the Gentlemen's Doubles title that year.

It would be the last Wimbledon for five years because of the First World War. Brookes's friend and rival Anthony Wilding – regarded as the world's first tennis superstar – was killed aged 31 at 4.45pm on 9 May 1915 when a shell exploded on top of the dugout he was in during the Battle of Aubers Ridge at Neuve-Chapelle, France. Three of the four occupants – two privates and Wilding – were killed. Only a young subaltern in the 4th Suffolks, Donald Pretty, survived.

Brookes, who suffered from stomach ulcers, was rejected for active military service. In August 1915, he became a commissioner for the Australian branch of the British Red Cross in Egypt serving until late 1916; he resigned in January 1917 and in May became commissioner for the British Red Cross in Mesopotamia. After the war, in 1919 and 1920, Brookes represented Australasia in Davis Cup matches – in total he played in 39 Davis Cup matches for Australia/New Zealand and the Australian Davis Cup team between 1905 and 1920 and was a member of the winning team in 1907, 1908, 1909, 1914, 1919. In 1924, he played for the last time at Wimbledon. Nicknamed "The Wizard", he was a shrewd tactician and a master strategist. Brookes was not a burly man and sometimes his stamina failed in long matches. Always immaculately turned out, he wore long-sleeved shirts and a peaked tweed cap and, for many years, used a heavy flat-top racquet with slack strings. In 1926, he became the first president of the Lawn Tennis Association of Australia, a post he held for the next 29 years until his retirement in June 1955. Unassuming, he could at times be outspokenly blunt, stubborn and uncompromising. The trophy presented to the Australian Open Men's Singles winners is called the Norman Brookes Challenge Cup. Knighted in 1939, he died on 28 September 1968 at his home, Elm Tree House, South Yarra, Victoria. He was 90.

FIRST
AUSTRALASIAN WIN IN DAVIS CUP
DWIGHT F. DAVIS INTERNATIONAL CHALLENGE CUP, WORPLE ROAD, WIMBLEDON, SURREY SW, ENGLAND. TUESDAY, 23 JULY 1907

Only the British Isles, the Australasians and the United States played in the 1907 Davis Cup. The opening ties between the Australasians and the United States took place at Wimbledon on 13–16 July 1907. A week after he became the first foreign winner of the Gentlemen's All-Comers' Singles at Wimbledon, Norman Brookes beat captain Beals C. Wright 6-4, 6-4, 6-2 before captain Anthony Wilding saw off Karl Behr of Yale 1-6, 6-3, 3-6, 7-5, 6-3 in the second singles match. Brookes and Wilding lost the doubles match to Wright and Behr 6-3, 10-12, 6-4, 2-6, 3-6. Brookes then beat Behr 4-6, 6-4, 6-1, 6-2. Wilding lost to Wright 8-6, 3-6, 3-6, 5-7 but it was enough to get Australasia a final place against the British Isles. In the first singles match of the final, Brookes easily saw off Arthur Gore 7-5, 6-1, 7-5. Anthony Wilding triumphed over Herbert Roper Barrett 1-6, 6-4, 6-3, 7-5. In the doubles match, Gore and Roper Barrett came from two sets behind to win 3-6, 4-6, 7-5, 6-2, 13-11. Gore beat Wilding in the third singles match – 3-6, 6-3, 7-5, 6-2 – leaving the final match to decide the competition. Norman Brookes added to his Wimbledon title with a comprehensive thrashing of Herbert Roper

Barrett 6-2, 6-0, 6-3 to take the Davis Cup Down Under for the first time. A contemporary account reported, "Watching this stern-jawed, imperturbable colonial [Brookes] on court, the onlooker might well get the impression that he never thaws – that life to him is a very serious occupation, trimmed with no frivolity or romance." Australasia retained the cup in 1908 and 1909, beating the United States on both occasions. Australia did not become an independent competitor in the Davis Cup until 1913, winning it that year.

DID YOU KNOW?
Karl Behr and R. Norris Williams both survived the sinking of *Titanic* in April 1912.

ONLY

WIMBLEDON GENTLEMEN'S
ALL-COMERS' SINGLES FINALIST
CONVICTED OF MURDER
Vere St Leger Goold, Palais de Justice, 5 Rue Colonel Bellando de Castro, 98000, Monte Carlo, Monaco. December 1907

Using the pseudonym "Mr St Leger", Irishman Vere St Leger Goold reached the final of the Gentlemen's All-Comers' Singles where, in something of a shock result, he lost in straight sets to the Reverend John Hartley, the only clergyman to win the title (see 1879) – probably as a result of sitting up all night drinking. Born into money at Clonmel, County Tipperary on 2 October 1853, the ambitious and flamboyant Goold showed skill at boxing as well as tennis. He eschewed the boxing ring for the tennis court and in June 1879 won the first Irish Lawn Tennis Championships (later the Irish Open) beating C.D. Barry 8-6, 8-6 in the final. The next month he entered the third Wimbledon and then the first open tournament held at Cheltenham, where he lost in the final to Willie Renshaw 4-6, 3-6, 6-5, 6-5, 4-6. At one stage in the final set he was 4-1 up. Popular with crowds, he had a ferocious backhand and played close to the net.

He lost the 1880 Irish Lawn Tennis Championships and gradually faded away from tennis. An avowed social climber, he decided to leave Ireland and move to London. A contemporary wrote, "Those who knew him described him as a man of perfect breeding and of courtly, charming manner, cultured and generous. He was wont when coming home late from the club or the theatre to collect stray cats and to bring them to share his supper." One day he met Marie Giraudin, a twice widowed Frenchwoman who owned a dressmaker's shop in Bayswater, west London. Crime historian Jay Robert Nash noted that "her first two husbands died mysteriously," adding that "there may have been more husbands who met the same fate".

They married in 1891 at St Mary of the Angels, Paddington, west London but both having expensive tastes, they quickly fell into debt. They emigrated to Montréal, the largest city in Canada's Québec province in 1897, where Marie opened another dressmaker's shop. Six years later, they moved to 18 Adelaide Terrace, Waterloo, Liverpool where they managed a laundry. They took to calling themselves "Sir Vere" and "Lady Goold". They moved to Monte Carlo, where they lived in a charming suite on the first floor of the Villa Menesini in the Boulevard des Moulin. Marie's niece, Isabelle, who had accompanied her uncle and aunt to Monaco, was rumoured to be a prostitute. Goold fancied himself as a big wheel at the roulette table and Marie was convinced she had a winning formula at the tables. They soon ran out of money. At the Monte Carlo Casino, they met the wealthy Emma Levin, the widow of Leopold Levin, a Stockholm broker. Marie quickly became Mrs Levin's BFF, but Mrs Levin was not the refined lady she appeared. Most evenings, after the roulette tables had closed at midnight, she would visit the cafés near the Place du Casino, where she would flash her diamonds, drink until the early hours, flirt, puff on cigarillos, and "make promiscuous acquaintances". Prior to her marriage, she had been in a children's home, and by the age of 17 she was on the police register of "loose women", and by 18 she had been taken to hospital with a dose of syphilis. Now a very merry widow, she decided to live it up on her husband's money.

However, Mrs Levin had another companion, Madame Castellazi, and she and Marie Goold loathed each other. One day, the two women had a stand-up row in the casino and ended up in the gossip columns. To avoid further bad publicity, Mrs Levin decided to leave the sunny place for shady people. She had loaned the Goolds £40 and wanted it back before she left. At 5pm on 4 August 1907, she went to their hotel suite where they bludgeoned and stabbed her to death – with a pestle, an Indian dagger and a butcher's knife – before dismembering her in the bathroom. When Mrs Levin did not return by midnight the next day, Madame Castellazi went to the police. They went to the Goolds' suite but they had already fled to Marseilles. En route to London, they stopped at a Marseilles hotel and left a large trunk at the local railway station. They booked in using the name of Mr and Mrs Javanach. A railway porter named Louis Pons noticed a revolting smell coming from the trunk and red liquid leaking from the bottom. The police were called and the trunk opened, to find the naked remains of Mrs Levin stuffed inside. The head and parts of the legs were missing. They were found in a small portmanteau which Goold was holding. Mrs Levin had several wounds to the head and she had been stabbed several times in the chest.

They were arrested and, at their trial, Mrs Goold at first incredibly claimed that when Mrs Levin visited her a man rushed in with a knife in his hand and killed her, as he shouted: "You wretch. You have ruined me. Now I am going to kill you." Goold stated that Mrs Levin was killed by a man when he and his wife were out and that they decided to cut the body in pieces and put them in a trunk in order to avoid scandal. Goold was described as amiable and clever, excellent company with a hobby of amateur photography. However, the truth came out during the course of the trial at Monaco's Palais de Justice and both were found guilty. She was sentenced to death on 4 December 1907 but no guillotine could be found in Monte Carlo, so in January 1908 the sentence was commuted to life in prison. He was sentenced to life in prison on Devil's Island. According to a reporter for *Paris Matin*, who met him on the island, the former tennis champion had become "a mere wreck, who takes solitary walks along the banks of the River Maroni, where for hours together he recites the memorials that he drew up for his defence, while the crocodiles doze in the water". On 8 September 1909, he committed suicide. He was 55. Marie Goold died of typhoid fever in a Montpellier jail in 1914. In 2011, a play about the case, *Love All*, was put on at the Clonmel Junction Festival.

FIRST
PLAYER TO WIN LADIES' SINGLES FINAL
AT WIMBLEDON IN THREE CONSECUTIVE YEARS

ONLY
GRAND SLAM WINNER AND
WOMEN'S AMATEUR GOLF CHAMPION

ONLY
GRAND SLAM WINNER TO WIN
OLYMPIC ARCHERY MEDAL

Lottie Dod, Ladies' Singles, The Championships, All England Lawn Tennis Club, Worple Road, Wimbledon, Surrey SW, England. Thursday, 9 July 1891 3.30pm; Ladies' Singles, The Championships, All England Lawn Tennis Club, Worple Road, Wimbledon, Surrey SW, England. Thursday, 7 July 1892; Ladies' Singles, The Championships, All England Lawn Tennis Club, Worple Road, Wimbledon, Surrey SW, England. Thursday, 20 July 1893; Women's Amateur Golf Championship, Troon Golf Club, Troon, Ayrshire KA10 6EP, Scotland. Friday, 13 May 1904; National Round Archery, Olympic Games, White City Stadium, London W12, England. Monday, 20 July 1908

Charlotte Dod was born on 24 September 1871 at Lower Bebington, Cheshire, into a wealthy sporting family. Her cotton broker and banker father, Joseph, died in November 1879 leaving enough money for his children not to have to worry about working. The Dods participated in many sports that were popular in the Victorian era, such as archery, billiards, bowls, croquet, golf and skating. Charlotte's elder sister, Ann, an accomplished skater, was regarded as one of England's best woman billiards players; on 18 July 1908 her eldest brother, William, won a gold medal for archery at the Olympic Games in London; and her second brother, Anthony, was chess champion of Cheshire and Lancashire. Lottie Dod began playing tennis when she was nine and entered a doubles competition with Ann at the Northern Championships, at Manchester Lawn Tennis Club in 1883. In the first round, they received a bye and were knocked out in the second round by Hannah Keith and Amber McCord, but won the consolation tournament.

In 1885, aged 13, Dod won all three open events at the Waterloo tournament and went close to beating the Wimbledon champion Maud Watson, who used a homemade oblong-shaped racquet in the finals of the Northern Championships, earning her the nickname "Little Wonder". In 1887, she won the Irish Nationals Singles Championship, beating Watson 6-4, 6-3. She entered the Ladies' Singles at The Championships for the first time in July 1887, aged 15 years and ten months. She made her way to the All-Comers' final where she beat Edith Cole 6-2, 6-3 before facing defending champion Blanche Bingley in the Challenge Round, which she won 6-2, 6-0 to take the Ladies' Singles title for the first time. *The Sheffield Independent* reported on 14 July 1887, "About the Ladies' Singles there is little to be said – only five entered as against eight last year. Miss Lottie Dod simply 'cantered' through the two rounds in which she had to play. In the final round she met Mrs C.J. Cole, formerly, as Miss Coleridge, well known as a tennis player. In the Challenge Round she easily vanquished Miss Bingley, who only got two games in the two sets."

The following year, with just one match to win to retain her title, Dod faced Blanche Bingley and took under 30 minutes to win 6-3, 6-3. In 1889, she took a yachting holiday and did not bother to defend her title. In 1890, she played no competitive tennis. In 1891, the title holder Lena Rice, the only winner of the Ladies' Singles championship from Ireland did not return to defend her title. Dod comprehensively double-bagelled Mrs Roberts in the quarter-final and then beat Bertha Steedman 6-3, 6-1 in the semi-final. In the final she met Bingley, now Mrs Hillyard, and won 6-2, 6-1. In 1892, Hillyard won the All-Comers' title and met Dod in the Challenge Round. Dod was taking no prisoners and won 6-1, 6-1. In 1893, again Dod faced Hillyard in the Challenge Round and lost the first set 8-6. However, Dod won the next two sets 6-1, 6-4 to take her fifth and third consecutive Wimbledon title.

Her game was based on footwork and anticipating what her opponent was going to do. After winning her fifth championship, 5ft 6½in Dod retired from tennis at the age of 21. She was said to be bored. To ease her way around court, Dod wore shorter skirts than were fashionable. She teamed these with black shoes and stockings and a white flannel cricket cap, which contrasted sharply with her jet-black hair. Tennis historian Elizabeth Wilson said, "Dod always spoke up in favour of the right of women to dress in a manner that did not impede their tennis." In doubles, she and her sister were among the first players to attack the net in tandem. "As a rule, ladies are too lazy at tennis," Dod said. "They should learn to run and run their hardest, too, not merely stride. They would find, if they tried, that many a ball, seemingly out of reach, could be returned with ease; but instead of running hard they go a few steps and exclaim, 'Oh, I can't' and stop."

Dod developed an interest in golf and entered the 1894 British Ladies' Championship but was knocked out in an early round. Golf was one of the few sports that did not come easily to her. With money no object, she spent the winter of 1895–1896 at St Moritz where she skied, went down the Cresta Run and, in February 1896, climbed the 13,130ft mountain Piz Zupo. In 1898, back in England, she lost in the semi-final of the British Ladies' Golf Championship at Great Yarmouth in Norfolk. In 1899, she was again beaten at the semi-final stage. A few days later, she beat the top Irishwoman, Jessie Magill, in an England versus Ireland international match. In 1904 Dod became the British National Golf champion. More than 6,000 (some sources say 5,000) spectators, including hundreds of dock workers who had left the Clyde, watched Dod beat May Hezlet by one hole at Troon. The same year, she played in the American Championship but was knocked out in the first round.

Adding to her portfolio of sporting achievements, in March 1899 she played at inside right for the England hockey team against Ireland at the Richmond Athletic Ground. Her skilful dribbling helped the home nation to a 3-1 win. In March 1900 at Ballsbridge, she scored both goals as England won 2-1.

In 1906, Dod turned her attention to archery. On 20 July 1908, at White City, she won a silver medal at the London Olympics. She lost by 46 points to Sybil "Queenie" Newall who, at 53, remains the oldest female medallist in Olympic history.

When the First World War broke out in August 1914, Dod took nursing qualifications but her sciatica meant she was refused a posting in France. She served at a military hospital near Newbury, Berkshire and was awarded a Red Cross gold medal. In 1921, she moved to London, where she became an accomplished singer. When the Second World War erupted in September 1939, she did not want to leave the capital during the Blitz but was persuaded to move to Westward Ho!, where she lived with her bachelor brother William. She returned to live in London in 1950, moving to Earls Court. She died, following a fall, at Birch Hill Nursing Home, Sway, Hampshire, on 27 June 1960. Her carer said that she was listening to Wimbledon on the wireless at the time.

FIRST
NON-AUSTRALIAN TO WIN
AUSTRALASIAN CHAMPIONSHIPS MEN'S SINGLES
FIRST
NON-AUSTRALIAN TO WIN
AUSTRALASIAN CHAMPIONSHIPS MEN'S DOUBLES

FRED ALEXANDER, MEN'S SINGLES, AUSTRALASIAN CHAMPIONSHIPS, DOUBLE BAY GROUNDS, SYDNEY, AUSTRALIA. SUNDAY, 13 DECEMBER 1908

Born at Sea Bright, New Jersey, in the United States, on 14 August 1880, Fred Alexander was educated at Princeton University. In December 1908, he became the first foreigner to win the Men's Doubles at the Australasian Championships before the biggest crowds ever seen at a lawn tennis match in Sydney. Teaming up with Victorian Alfred Dunlop, they beat G.G. Sharp and Anthony Wilding 6-3, 6-2, 6-1. Later that same day, he became the first foreigner to win the Men's Singles at the Australasian Championships, beating Alfred Dunlop 3-6, 3-6, 6-0, 6-2, 6-3. Later that month, he was part of the American team that lost to Australasia at the Albert Ground, Melbourne in the Davis Cup. Alexander lost both his singles matches against Norman Brookes and Anthony Wilding as well as the doubles match against these two, together with his partner Beals Wright. Alexander was inducted into the International Tennis Hall of Fame in 1961. He died at Beverly Hills, California on 3 March 1969, aged 88.

FIRST
BRITON TO WIN
AUSTRALASIAN CHAMPIONSHIPS

FIRST
AUSTRALASIAN CHAMPIONSHIPS
WITH TWO BRITISH FINALISTS
James Cecil Parke and Alfred Beamish, Men's Singles, Australasian Championships, Hastings, New Zealand. Wednesday, 1 January 1913

The distance to Australia meant that usually only Australian and New Zealand players took part in the Australasian Championships, so the winners of most of the early titles were players from that region (but see 1908). In the 1912 Championships (held from 30 December 1912 until 1 January 1913), the reigning champion Norman Brookes chose not to defend his title and New Zealand player Anthony Wilding did not return from Europe to compete. There were eight competitors and four were British and the remaining were New Zealanders. It was **the first time that the Australasian Championships had been held in Hastings** and the second time (of eight) in New Zealand. In the first round, Parke despatched fellow Briton A. Lowe after being two sets to love down. He came back to win 4-6, 2-6, 6-1, 6-0, 6-4. In the quarter-final, he beat New Zealander Geoffrey Ollivier in straight sets 6-1, 6-4, 8-6. His semi-final opponent was New Zealander Robert Swanston and Parke won 6-2, 6-2, 6-3. Briton Alfred Beamish was Parke's final contestant and the match swung both ways with Beamish twice leading, but Parke won 3-6, 6-3, 1-6, 6-1, 7-5. Alfred Beamish was also on the losing side in the all-British final in the Men's Doubles. Parke combined with Charles Dixon to beat Beamish and Gordon Lowe 6-4, 6-4, 6-2.

ONLY
TITANIC SURVIVOR TO WIN A
GRAND SLAM TOURNAMENT

R. NORRIS WILLIAMS, UNITED STATES NATIONAL CHAMPIONSHIPS, NEWPORT CASINO, 186-202 BELLEVUE AVENUE, NEWPORT, RHODE ISLAND 02840, UNITED STATES OF AMERICA. MONDAY, 26 AUGUST 1912

At 2.20am on Monday, 15 April 1912, RMS *Titanic* sank, two and a half hours after she struck an iceberg. Of a total of 2,224 passengers, 1,517 were lost, mainly due to hypothermia, although the first news story was headlined, "All Saved From Titanic After Collision". In the last few minutes the "unsinkable" 882-feet long *Titanic* stood almost perpendicular out of the water. She was carrying the regulation 16 lifeboats, only enough to carry 1,178 people to safety. Six years earlier, one of the passengers, W.T. Stead, a celebrated journalist, had written a story 'From the Old World' to the *New* about a terrifying transatlantic journey through icebergs. He wrote, "The ocean bed beneath the run of the liners is strewn with whitening bones of thousands who have taken their passages as we have done, but who never saw their destination." Stead never saw his destination.

One who did was an American Richard Norris Williams, more commonly known as R. Norris "Dick" Williams. He was born on 29 January 1891, in Geneva, Switzerland, the son of Duane Williams, a direct descendant of Benjamin Franklin, and Lydia Biddle White who hailed from Philadelphia. Williams began playing tennis in 1903 and eight years later won the Swiss Championship. In April 1912, *Williams père et fils*, decided to go back to America to see Lydia. Both men boarded RMS *Titanic* at Cherbourg travelling first class. When she hit the iceberg, Dick Williams smashed down a door to rescue a trapped passenger and was threatened with a fine by a White Star Line steward for damaging company property. Williams stayed on deck until almost the end when he and his father were washed overboard by a wave. Duane died when he was hit by a falling funnel but Dick survived. He was wearing a fur coat when he went into the water. He threw it off along with his shoes. He clung to partially submerged lifeboat Collapsible A before dragging himself onboard. Eventually, those on the Collapsible A were moved to Lifeboat 14 and finally the rescue ship RMS *Carpathia* arrived and began uploading the survivors. Williams was suffering from extreme frostbite in his legs and the *Carpathia* surgeon wanted to amputate them to save Williams's life. Williams refused and saved his legs by the simple expedience of standing up every two hours and going for a walk.

His "treatment" worked, because later that year he won the Mixed Doubles at the United States Championships – with Mary Browne, he beat Eleonora Sears and William Clothier 6-4, 2-6, 11-9. In 1912, he went to Harvard and won the Intercollegiate Singles Tennis Championship (1913 and 1915). White Star Line also returned his fur coat.

On 1 September 1914 and in 1916, Williams won the US National Championships, beating Maurice McLoughlin and Bill Johnston respectively in the final; he won the Mixed Doubles at Wimbledon in 1920; he won an Olympic gold medal in 1924 (despite a sprained ankle); the same year he was a semi-finalist in the Gentlemen's Singles at Wimbledon and in 1925 and 1926 he won the Mixed Doubles at the US National Championships. He was 44 when he retired from championship tennis. He was inducted into the International Tennis Hall of Fame (Newport, Rhode Island) in 1957. He died of emphysema on 2 June 1968 at Bryn Mawr, Pennsylvania, aged 77.

FIRST

AMERICAN TO WIN
GENTLEMEN'S SINGLES AT WIMBLEDON

BILL TILDEN, GENTLEMEN'S SINGLES, THE CHAMPIONSHIPS, WORPLE ROAD, WIMBLEDON, SURREY SW, ENGLAND. SATURDAY, 3 JULY 1920

The man who would dominate men's world tennis in the 1920s was born William Tatem Tilden II at Overleigh, his parents' mansion in Germantown, Philadelphia. They were a wealthy household, but Tilden suffered from depression aged 22 when his father William Tatem Tilden, a wool merchant and local politician, died on 29 July 1915, aged 60. Tilden had begun playing tennis aged six or seven at the Onteora (NY) club near the family summer house in the Catskill Mountains and it was to tennis he turned in his depression. In 1911 he won his first tournaments – the Germantown Junior Singles and Doubles titles. Two years later, he won his first national title – the Mixed Doubles Championships with Mary Kendall Browne and they successfully defended the title in 1914. In 1918 and 1919 at the US National Championships he lost to Robert Lindley Murray and "Little Bill" Johnston, respectively in straight sets. The following year, he was back and won the Men's Singles at the US National Championships and retained the title in 1921, 1922, 1923, 1924 and 1925 (and again in 1929).

In 1920, he sailed for Europe and Wimbledon. In the first round he easily saw off the Briton H.R. Fussell 6-3, 6-2, 6-1. Another Briton, S. Franklin, caused no more difficulty for Tilden, going down 6-1, 6-1, 6-0. In the third round Tilden played James Cecil Parke, a sporting renaissance man. Tilden saw him off 6-3, 6-2, 6-4. Algy Kingscote gave Tilden more of a challenge in the fourth round taking him to five sets. The big American, however, triumphed 6-3, 5-7, 6-4, 5-7, 6-3. In the quarter-finals, Tilden faced his fifth Briton, Randolph Lycett. The first set went to Tilden 7-5, but Lycett pulled back the second 6-4. Tilden held his nerve and won the third and fourth sets 6-4, 7-5 to win the match and progress to the semi-final. His opponent was the American Chuck Garland (who would win the Gentlemen's Doubles at Wimbledon that year). Tilden saw him off in straight sets 6-4, 8-6, 6-2. In the All-Comers' final Tilden met the Japanese Zenzo Shimizu and Tilden won 6-4, 6-4, 13-11 despite being behind 4-1 in the first set, 4-2 in the second and 5-2 in the third. He then went on to face the reigning champion Australian Gerald Patterson. At the start of the most successful decade of his career, Tilden could do no wrong and beat the Antipodean 2-6, 6-3, 6-2, 6-4.

The author Paul Gallico wrote, "To his opponent it was a contest; with Tilden it was an expression of his own tremendous and overwhelming ego, coupled with feminine vanity." Was the latter remark a less than subtle dig at Tilden's homosexuality? As he travelled around the world, Tilden's entourage always contained a ball boy, usually a German. Tilden and the boy would travel in one car while everyone else piled into two other vehicles. On trains, Tilden would share a sleeper with his favoured boy. Often his young boyfriends would steal from him but he was a generous benefactor giving one catamite a watch worth $1,500. As he got older and his tennis career faded, Tilden turned to teenage boys for sex. Just before 10pm on 23 November 1946 on Sunset Boulevard, two policemen saw a 1942 Packard Clipper being badly driven. They looked closely and were surprised to see a boy in the driver's seat with an older man beside him with one arm around the boy's shoulders "holding him very tightly, and it appeared, with his right hand in the boy's lap". They pulled the car over at the junction of North Rexford Drive and the man – Tilden – quickly swapped places with Bobby, his young companion. The police ordered the boy from the car and as he got out they noticed his flies were undone. Tilden was arrested by the Beverly Hills police and charged with a misdemeanour ("contributing to the delinquency of a minor") for soliciting an underage male, a 14-year-old boy with whom he was having sex in a moving vehicle. Tilden was taken to the police station and signed a statement without reading it. When he realised he might actually be in a spot of bother, Tilden called Jerry Giesler, the famed Hollywood lawyer, but the man who had represented Clarence Darrow, Charles Chaplin, Alexander Pantages (three times), Errol Flynn, Busby Berkeley, film producer Walter Wanger, gangster Bugsy Siegel, and Marilyn Monroe wanted nothing to do with Bill Tilden. Tilden went to a young lawyer named Richard Maddox, who took the case, albeit reluctantly, and said, "The toughest cases I've ever had are where a dog or a child are the victims."

Tilden became increasingly uncooperative with his lawyer. It took him some time to admit to Maddox what had really happened and explained that he had been through these little local difficulties before and they had all been made to go away. "But Bill," said Maddox, "this time you're indicted. They're going to hang you. They're going to chew headlines." Tilden was a friend of Charlie Chaplin and assumed he would pull strings. Maddox went to see Chaplin, whose advice to Tilden was that he should skip bail and flee the country. Maddox learned from Tilden that Bobby was no innocent. On the day he had had sex with Tilden, Bobby had slept with a girl his own age. As things heated up, Tilden asked Bobby where he had learned so much about sex – "In the private school I just left," was his reply. It was not the first time the two had been intimate. They had met at the Los Angeles Tennis Club and went out to dinner that night at Eaton's on La Cienaga Boulevard. They repaired to Tilden's car for sex and then Bobby had the tennis giant drive him home via his school in Westwood, so Tilden would know from where to collect Bobby the following Wednesday. The following Saturday, Tilden picked up Bobby from his girlfriend's house on Lucerne Avenue at 5.45pm. They went to dinner at Castle Steak House on Vermont Avenue before going to the Pantages cinema to see *The Jolson Story*. It was after the film in the car home that the police got involved.

Maddox got letters of good character from 15 of Tilden's friends. Some even lied and said Tilden's fling with Bobby was a one-off. The court-appointed social worker said that he thought Tilden should be treated and not jailed. The judge, A.A. Scott, however, had long heard rumours that Tilden was a practising homosexual with a predilection for small boys. On 16 January 1947 at 9.30am, Tilden turned up to court for sentencing, fully expecting his status and Hollywood connections would save him from prison. Tilden told the judge, "I very deeply regret the incident. I have had a terrible lesson, one which I will never forget." He sat back and waited for the slap on the wrists. The judge looked at him and said, "I am just wondering, Mr Tilden, have you ever given any thought … to the harm you could do if you were ever caught doing something like this?" Tilden replied, "Sir, I don't think I have thought of that because I have never been involved in anything of the kind." Judge

Scott remarked, "You mean by that you were never caught?" Tilden lied again. "I mean I was not involved in it, sir. In that kind of thing. Years ago, sir, I was once very stupid, but in recent years I have not been involved."

The judge was stupefied at Tilden's brazen untruthfulness in his court. He began discussing the case and then suddenly said, "All right, the court at this time is going to sentence you to the county jail for a period of one year." As Tilden slumped in his chair, Maddox leapt out of his, asking the judge for a stay, but Mr Scott refused and Maddox had to help the shocked Tilden to his feet so he could be led away to jail by the Los Angeles Sheriff's Department. After a week in a regular jail, Tilden, prisoner number 9413, was transferred to Castaic Honor Farm, an open prison. Tilden served seven and a half months and was released on 30 August 1947. As part of his release, Tilden was forbidden from associating with any minors.

Charlie Chaplin stood by Tilden as did the Joseph Cottens and David O. Selznick but many of the Hollywood glitterati turned their back on their friend. On the morning of 28 January 1949, Tilden was spotted at the corner of Westwood Boulevard and Wilshire Boulevard picking up a 16-year-old hitchhiker named Michael Schachel, a grocery clerk, in breach of his parole. He was arrested that afternoon at his home. At the hearing Michael said that as they drove Tilden tried to slip his hand inside the boy's trousers. Charlie Chaplin sent an emissary to the court, offering to take Tilden out of the country for the rest of his probation and keep an eye on him. It was a non-starter. Another homosexual tennis player, Coco Gentien, urged Tilden to come and live in France. Tilden was too patriotic to consider the suggestion. Tilden went to see Judge Scott and asked him to sentence him so he could come out with a clean slate and return to spending time with his young friends. He begged the judge to not keep him away from children. "Judge, I can't help myself," said Tilden. The judge asked him whether psychiatric treatment would help. "It doesn't do any good, nor would any more do any good." On 10 February 1949, his 56th birthday, Tilden was sent back to prison for a year. He was released on 18 December 1949 in time for Christmas.

On 3 February 1950, Tilden was named the Greatest Tennis Player of the first half of the century in an Associated Press poll of sports journalists, despite "the personal tragedy which has befallen the great champion in recent years". He had received ten times more votes than his nearest rival. Out of jail, Tilden hoped to resume his tennis career. He entered the 1953 US Professional Championships at Ohio's Lakewood Park. On 5 June, the night before he was due to leave for the tournament, he suffered a heart attack in his apartment at 2025 North Argyle Avenue and died. He was buried at his family's burial plot at the Ivy Hill Cemetery in Germantown. Tennis writer Bud Collins said, "Nobody had a more devastating service than Tilden's cannonball, or a more challenging second serve than his kicking American twist. No player had a stronger combination of forehand and backhand drives, supplemented by a forehand chop and backhand slice."

ONLY
WIMBLEDON PLAYER WHO DRANK
CHAMPAGNE DURING A MATCH
RANDOLPH LYCETT, GENTLEMEN'S SINGLES, THE CHAMPIONSHIPS, WORPLE ROAD, WIMBLEDON, SURREY SW, ENGLAND. SATURDAY, 25 JUNE 1921

Birmingham-born and Australia-raised Randolph Lycett was best known for his doubles play although he was the runner-up at the 1922 Wimbledon Gentlemen's Singles (losing to Gerald Patterson). The previous year, he had reached the quarter-final without losing a set (first round: L.E. Gaunt 6-0, 6-2, 6-4; second round Arthur Belgrave 6-3, 6-2, 6-4; third round Ulysses Williams 6-2, 6-2, 6-0; fourth round Alfred Beamish 8-6, 8-6, 6-4). In the quarter-final he was drawn against his first non-British opponent, the Japanese Zenzo Shimizo. Like Lycett, Schmidzu had not dropped a set on his way to the match. Indeed, he had dropped only four games in his first two matches at The Championships.

Schmidzu was known to the Worple Road faithful as "the little Japanese" and they enjoyed his unorthodox style of play and the pork pie hat he invariably wore.

The quarter-final was played on the middle Saturday of the tournament and it was an exceptionally hot day. The "stands reflect the heat and keep off any breeze" reported *The Times*, adding, "In England the game is supposed to be played without break from start to finish though it is an accepted convention that a player may wipe his brow or moisten his gusset as he passes the umpire's chair." In other words, the players had to get on with it once they stepped on court – no breaks, no chairs (they arrived in 1975), no Robinsons Barley Water (that made its debut in 1948; the company sent 960 free bottles to the tournament each year), and no ball boys wafting towels at a player's fevered brow.

Schmidzu won the first set 6-3. Lycett hit back, winning the second and third 11-9 and 6-3. During the third set, Lycett drank gin each time the players changed ends. It did not appear to be enough for him. In the fourth set, he was in need of sustenance and ordered a bottle of champagne. The *Daily Telegraph* reported that "Lycett broke all precedent by bringing a 'trainer' onto the Centre Court, equipped with champagne". The champagne had a double effect on Lycett – it made him even more dehydrated but also freed him to not care what kind of shots he was playing. He made some appalling mistakes but also some cracking returns. "Mr Lycett's distress was obvious," said another report. "He was still capable of making powerful smashes but fell over several times when trying to turn sharply." Lycett called for another bottle and this was delivered by a liveried waiter from the nearby refreshment tent. Schmidzu took the fourth set 6-2 and Lycett took to sipping from a hip flask that was said to contain brandy. "In the last set all one noticed were the delays," wrote one journalist, "but no sign of impatience from Mr Schmidzu as he waited with polite concern while applications internal and external were administered to Mr Lycett." At one stage in the fifth set, 5ft 8in Lycett had two match points but was unable to seal the deal and the Japanese took the fifth set 10-8. Lycett died aged only 48 in Jersey on 9 February 1935.

LAST

GENTLEMEN'S SINGLES
CHALLENGE ROUND WINNER AT WIMBLEDON

LAST

WIMBLEDON CHAMPIONSHIPS
HELD AT WORPLE ROAD

BILL TILDEN, GENTLEMEN'S SINGLES CHALLENGE ROUND, THE CHAMPIONSHIPS, WORPLE ROAD, WIMBLEDON, SURREY SW, ENGLAND. SATURDAY, 2 JULY 1921

From 1878 until 1921 the winner of Wimbledon was decided by a match between the winner of the All-Comers' tournament and the previous year's champion, known as the Challenge Round. In 1921, Brian Norton – known as Babe – from South Africa fought his way through the All-Comers' competition. In the first round he played four sets against John Cecil Masterman and won 6-4, 6-4, 10-12, 6-2. His second-round opponent was the Briton Basil Harrison and he beat him relatively comfortably 6-3, 6-2, 6-1. In the third round Norton beat the Natal-born Englishman Patrick Wheatley 6-4, 6-4, 6-3. His fourth-round opponent was Indian Sydney Jacob who was no match for him, going down 6-1, 6-1, 6-2. Canadian Henry Mayes was the quarter-final challenger and he beat Norton 6-4 in the first set but lost the next three sets 6-2, 6-2, 6-2. The future Olympic gold medal winner Frank Hunter, an American, played Norton in the semi-finals. Norton went two sets up, 6-0, 6-3, before Hunter fought back to level, winning the third and fourth sets 7-5, 7-5, but then Norton took the fifth and final set 6-2. In the final, Norton met the first Spaniard to make a name for himself on the tennis circuit, Manuel Alonso. The Spaniard took the first two sets 7-5, 6-4 and looked set to win the All-Comers' competition but Norton had other ideas and fought back to win the remaining three sets 7-5, 6-3, 6-3.

Having won the All-Comers' competition, Norton had to face the previous year's champion Bill Tilden in the Challenge Round for the ultimate prize. Tilden had left America in May 1921 aboard the *Mauretania* and arrived in France, where he played on clay. Tilden was under the weather after almost a year of playing and touring and came down with a case of boils. They were removed during an operation in Paris. Disembarking in London, he booked into a nursing home for three weeks to recuperate from his "indisposition". Tilden was still in bed when what was to be the last Wimbledon at Worple Road began on 20 June 1921. Indeed, he did not get out of bed until five days before he had to face Norton in the final.

Norton, the South African, was a crowd favourite and they went wild when he shot to a two-set lead 6-4, 6-2. In the third set, Tilden changed his usual hard-hitting game and began chopping and slicing the ball and soon he was three games up. Norton was not able to counter Tilden's new game play and lost the third set 6-1. The crowd began booing the big American, who continued chopping and slicing the ball. The match referee tried to quiet the crowd by saying that Tilden was playing quite legally but they were having none of it and the cat-calling and jeering continued. Tilden won the fourth set 6-0. Tilden noted: "[Norton] simply threw away the fourth set from sheer nerves." In the final set, Norton took a 5-4 lead and then got to 40-15 – two Championship points. Tilden pulled back to 30-40 but then hit a shot long and knew it was going out, so he began to run towards the net to congratulate Norton on his victory. On seeing the American approach the net, the South African thought he was going to volley and so hit the ball that was going out himself, making the score deuce. The American needed no more help and won the final set – and the Championship – 7-5. Tilden made his way back to the dressing room where he fainted. Norton is one of only two men to hold a championship point in a Grand Slam Gentlemen's Singles final and yet not win a title (the other was Guillermo Coria at the 2004 French Open). In 1923, with Tilden as his partner, Norton would win the Men's Doubles title at the US National Championships. It would not be until 2018 – 97 years later – that another South African citizen, Kevin Anderson, would reach the Gentlemen's Singles final at Wimbledon.

DID YOU KNOW?

Sir John Cecil Masterman's best performance at Wimbledon was reaching the fourth round in 1923. He achieved many other distinctions, including becoming Vice-Chancellor of the University of Oxford and running the Double-Cross System, which controlled double agents in Britain during the Second World War. A book he wrote on the System was banned in Britain and had to be published in the United States. He died on 6 June 1977, aged 86.

LAST
LADIES' SINGLES CHALLENGE ROUND
WINNER AT WIMBLEDON

Suzanne Lenglen, Ladies' Singles Challenge Round, The Championships, Worple Road, Wimbledon, Surrey SW, England. July 1921

On 5 July 1919 (in the longest Wimbledon final to that date, 10-8, 4-6, 9-7) and again in 1920, French tennis superstar Suzanne Lenglen won the Ladies' Singles title at Wimbledon, on both occasions beating Briton Dorothea Lambert Chambers. Lenglen was known for her flamboyant, demonstrative manner and her outfits with bare forearms and calf-length dresses that were considered revealing for the time. She was also known to sip brandy between sets of her matches.

In 1920, Lenglen had only had to play one game to retain her Wimbledon title but 1921 was the last time that arrangement was in place. In that year, Elizabeth Ryan beat Phyllis Satterthwaite 6-1, 6-0 in the All-Comers' final but then lost to Lenglen 6-2, 6-0 in the last ladies Challenge Round.

ONLY
MAN TO MAKE A CENTURY AT LORD'S, WIN OLYMPIC GOLD MEDAL,

WIN DOUBLES AT WIMBLEDON,
AND CAPTAIN THE ENGLAND FOOTBALL TEAM

Max Woosnam, Men's Doubles, Olympics, Antwerp, Belgium. August 1920; Gentlemen's Doubles, The Championships, Worple Road, Wimbledon, Surrey SW, England. July 1921; Davis Cup, Allegheny Country Club, 250 Country Club Road, Sewickley, Pennsylvania 15143, United States of America. Thursday, 4 – Saturday, 6 August 1921; England v Wales, Anfield, Anfield Road, Liverpool L4 0TH, England. Monday, 13 March 1922

Born in Liverpool on 6 September 1892, the son of a clergyman, Max Woosnam was one of the greatest sportsman Britain has ever produced. Educated at Winchester, he scored 144 and 33 not out playing for a Public Schools XI against the4 MCC. In 1911, Woosnam went to Cambridge University where he became a quadruple Blue, representing the university at cricket, football, tennis, real tennis and golf. In 1919, Woosnam was a finalist in the 1919 All England Plate competition held at Wimbledon for players who had been knocked out in the first or second rounds. In April 1919, Woosnam played for Cambridge University against Queen's Club. *The Times* reported, "Woosnam is a player of many games, and he could excel at tennis if he could devote enough time to the game … tennis is a mistress who must be constantly wooed." In 1920 he won a gold medal at the Olympics. In 1921, he and Randolph Lycett won the Gentlemen's Doubles at the Wimbledon Championships beating Arthur Lowe and James Cecil Parke 6-3, 6-0, 7-5 in the All-Comers' final after the reigning champions, Chuck Garland and R. Norris Williams, did not defend their title. With Phyllis Howkins, he was a runner-up in the Mixed Doubles losing 6-3, 6-1 to Randolph Lycett and Elizabeth Ryan.

Two years later, he was a quarter-finalist at the Gentlemen's Singles at Wimbledon.

On the football pitch from 1914 until 1926, he played at centre-half for Corinthian, Chelsea, Manchester City (making his debut on 1 January 1920 and captaining the side to a runners-up place in Division One in 1920/1921) and Northwich Victoria (making his debut on 25 December 1924). On 13 March 1922, he played his only game for England against Wales and captained the side. A heavy smoker all his life, he died, aged 72, of respiratory failure on 14 July 1965.

FIRST

BALLOT FOR TICKETS AT WIMBLEDON

The Championships, Centre Court, Church Road, Wimbledon, Surrey SW, England. Monday, 26 June – Saturday, 10 July 1922

So many people wanted to attend the first Championships at Wimbledon's new home a ballot system was instigated. It proved so popular that the system has been adopted for every championship since.

FIRST

MATCH PLAYED ON CENTRE COURT, WIMBLEDON

Major Algy Kingscote v Leslie Godfree, Gentlemen's Singles, The Championships, Centre Court, Church Road, Wimbledon, Surrey SW, England. Monday, 26 June 1922

By 1914, it was decided that the facilities at Worple Road did not meet the requirements of people wanting to watch tennis. Following the end of the First World War, a search was undertaken for nearby land where the Wimbledon Championships could move to. On 23 June 1920, the All England Lawn Tennis Ground Ltd was established to buy the land for the new venue. Once the land was bought for £7,870 (£400,000 at 2020 prices), architect Captain Stanley Peach was hired to design a Centre Court plus offices and facilities. The enterprise between the All England Club and the Lawn Tennis Association cost £140,000 (£6,750,000 at 2020 values) and was paid for by the issuing of £50 (£2,500, 2020) debentures that could be redeemed in 1947. At the time many predicted that the idea would be a waste of time and money and there was no need for a venue for 13,500 spectators.

At 3pm on 26 June 1922, the National Anthem was played and HM King George V opened the new stadium. Accompanied by HM Queen Mary, resplendent in a hat of dark straw and a fox fur over her shoulders, the king sat down to watch the tennis. It then began to rain – it turned out to be the wettest fortnight in the tournament's history – but on that first day the rain eased up and a gong sounded and a retinue of groundsmen and boys pulled back the tarpaulin covering the turf specially imported from the Solway Firth and a cheer went up from the crowd. The first match was played between Major Algy Kingscote and Leslie Godfree. Serving first, Godfree deliberately hit the initial two deliveries into the net and then rushed forward to put the first ball in his pocket as a souvenir. His son said he kept it until it disintegrated with age.

Kingscote won the first game but then suffered some difficulty with his returns and ceded a game to Godfree, before pulling himself together and winning the first set 6-1. The second set started out as an equal battle but Kingscote managed to win 6-3 despite slipping several times on the greasy surface. Kingscote regained his form in the third set and thanks to some delightful passing shots he took the third set 6-0 and the match 3-0. Kingscote reached the fourth round of the tournament that year. No games were played on the other courts that day and the only other match on Centre Court was the start of the doubles match between Briton Walter Crawley and American A.W. Asthalter and Briton Arthur Gore and Australian Frank Riseley. Rain interrupted the match at the end of the first set, by which time the King and Queen had left. The final score was 6-2, 6-2, 6-4.

Centre Court – the most important and respected court at the ground – gets its name because at the original site on Worple Road, the main court was constructed in the centre and the other courts built around it. At Church Road, the name did not reflect its geography until, in 1980, additional courts were built and Centre Court ended up in the middle.

DID YOU KNOW?

Above the players' entrance to Centre Court at Wimbledon is a quotation from the poem "If" by Rudyard Kipling. "If you can meet with triumph and disaster and treat those two impostors just the same."

FIRST

LADIES' SINGLES WINNER AT
WIMBLEDON AFTER CHALLENGE ROUND ABOLISHED
SUZANNE LENGLEN, LADIES' SINGLES, THE CHAMPIONSHIPS, CHURCH ROAD, WIMBLEDON, SURREY SW, ENGLAND.
SATURDAY, 8 JULY 1922

Whether she played one game to beat the All-Comers' winner or had to go through the whole tournament, Suzanne Lenglen was almost unbeatable. In the first round in 1922 she got a double bagel against South African Mrs M.F. Ellis. In the second round, she beat Kitty McKane in straight sets 6-1, 7-5. Another double bagel was the result of the third-round match between Lenglen and Evelyn Colyer. In the quarter-final, Lenglen beat Elizabeth Ryan 6-1, 8-6, then in the semi-final, she faced Irene Peacock from South Africa and won 6-4, 6-1. In the final she was up against Norway-born Molla Mallory who had become a naturalised American. Lenglen took just 26 minutes to beat Mallory 6-2, 6-0 – the shortest final in a Grand Slam tournament on record.

It was to be Mallory's only Wimbledon Singles final but she won the Singles title at the US Championships a record eight times in 15 attempts, with the last of her titles occurring at age 42 in 1926. She won in 1915, 1916, 1917, 1918, 1920, 1921, 1922 and 1926. In the days long before women grunted as loudly as possible when they strike the ball, Mallory was a hard hitter. She said, "I find that the girls generally do not hit the ball as hard as they should. I believe in always hitting the ball with all my might, but there seems to be a disposition to 'just get it over' in many girls whom I have played. I do not call this tennis."

On her way to winning the 1921 US National Championships, she beat Lenglen in the second round at Forest Hills. She was given some advice by Bill Tilden before the match and that was to "hit the cover off the ball". In the first set Mallory was two games to love and 40-0 up when Lenglen began coughing. Mallory won the first set 6-2 and was leading 40-0 on Lenglen's serve in the first game of the second set when the Frenchwoman began to cry. She wandered over to the umpire's chair and speaking in her native tongue told him that she was too ill to continue. As the two women left the court, there were boos from the 8,000-strong crowd – the largest attendance for a women's tennis match at that time. After the match, the United States Tennis Association accused Lenglen of pretending to be ill. The French Tennis Federation (FTF) announced that it accepted Lenglen's explanation. Not everyone in the French tennis authorities believed her, however. Albert de Joannis, the vice president of the FTF was with Lenglen on her trip to the United States and he left his job over the FTF decision. He said Lenglen had merely been "defeated by a player who on that date showed a better brand of tennis". Indeed, Lenglen continued to attend parties and appeared at Forest Hills the next day. It has been suggested that Lenglen was suffering from period pain but that was never publicly discussed at the time as it was a strictly taboo subject.

After retaining her Wimbledon title in 1922, Lenglen is reported to have said to her opponent, "Now, Mrs Mallory, I have proved to you today what I could have done to you in New York last year." Mallory is said to have stated, "Mlle Lenglen, you have done to me today what I did to you in New York last year; you have beaten me." The media played up a rivalry between the two women that both said did not exist. Mallory said, "The newspapers are the dirtiest, filthiest things that ever happened. I don't want my name in the newspapers. I have a better chance on the courts than in the newspapers of my own country."

Mallory is the only woman apart than Chris Evert to have won the US Championships four consecutive times. She died on 22 November 1959, aged 75, in Stockholm, Sweden. Lenglen would win the Wimbledon Ladies' Singles on two more occasions – 1923 and 1925. She was rated the 24th greatest player of all time by the Tennis Channel and was the ninth-highest-ranked woman overall, as well as the highest-ranked woman to play exclusively in the amateur era. She won 250 titles made up of 83 in singles, 74 in doubles, and 93 in mixed doubles. In June 1938 Lenglen was diagnosed with leukaemia. Three weeks later, she went blind. She died, aged 39, on 4 July 1938, of pernicious anaemia. She was buried in the Cimetière de Saint-Ouen at Saint-Ouen near Paris. In 1978, Lenglen was inducted into the International Tennis Hall of Fame.

FIRST

GENTLEMEN'S SINGLES WINNER AT WIMBLEDON AFTER CHALLENGE ROUND ABOLISHED

GERALD PATTERSON, GENTLEMEN'S SINGLES, THE CHAMPIONSHIPS, CHURCH ROAD, WIMBLEDON, SURREY SW, ENGLAND. MONDAY, 10 JULY 1922

From 1878 until 1921 the Wimbledon champions only had to win one match to retain their crown – beating the winner of the All-Comers' competition. Gerald Patterson was **the first champion who had to play the entire tournament to win** – the 1921 champion Bill Tilden did not return to defend his title so the winner of the tournament did not have to play another game against the previous champion.

Gerald Leighton Patterson was born on 17 December 1895 at Preston, Melbourne – his maternal aunt was the opera singer Dame Nellie Melba. He won the Schoolboys' Singles championship in 1911 and 1913 and was coached by Norman Brookes (see 1907). In 1914, he was runner-up in the Australian Singles and won the Doubles title. During the First World War, he was awarded the Military Cross in 1917 for bravery at Messines. In 1919, he won Wimbledon's Gentlemen's Singles, beating his mentor Brookes in the Challenge Round 6-3, 7-5, 6-2, having won the All-Comers' final against Algy Kingscote. Brookes had won in the last Wimbledon before the Great War, beating Anthony Wilding.

In the 1922 competition, Patterson got off to a good start when he got a walkover against his first-round opponent Britain's D. L. Morgan. In the second round, he beat the American Axel Gravem 6-1, 6-1, 6-4. In the third round he beat the future Musketeer Jean Borotra 6-0, 6-1, 6-3. In the fourth round he came up against Algy Kingscote and the match went to five sets. Patterson won 6-4, 3-6, 5-7, 6-4, 6-3. In the quarter-final Patterson played Briton Cecil Campbell and beat him 7-9, 6-3, 6-2, 6-1 to progress to the semi-final. His opponent there was fellow Australian James Anderson. It also went to five sets with Patterson triumphing 6-1, 3-6, 7-9, 6-1, 6-3. In the final, Patterson met Randolph Lycett and won in straight sets 6-3, 6-4, 6-2. It was his second and last Championship at Wimbledon. He represented and captained Australasia in the Davis Cup in 1919, 1920 and 1922, and Australia in 1924, 1925 and 1928. He used brute strength rather than subtlety on the court and in the 1925 Davis Cup match against France he knocked Jean Borotra unconscious with a powerful smash. Patterson retired from tennis in 1928 but in 1946, weighing 18 stone, led the Davis Cup team as non-playing captain. Patterson died in Mornington Hospital on 13 June 1967 and was cremated.

━◆◆◆◆◆━

FIRST

SISTERS TO PLAY IN LADIES' DOUBLES FINAL AT WIMBLEDON

KITTY MCKANE AND MARGARET STOCKS, LADIES' DOUBLES, THE CHAMPIONSHIPS, CHURCH ROAD, WIMBLEDON, SURREY SW, ENGLAND. WEDNESDAY, 12 JULY 1922

The 1922 Championships were memorable for many firsts. The sisters Kitty McKane and Margaret Stocks were born in London in 1896 and 1895. In 1921, Margaret became the first sister to marry when she married Andrew Denys Stocks. That same year, she and Kitty won the All England Women's Doubles badminton title. They won the title again in 1924 and Stocks won the Singles Championship in 1925. The sisters were also tennis aces and in 1922, they reached the final of the Ladies' Doubles. In the first round, they beat Sylvia Lumley-Ellis and M.S. Scott 6-2, 6-2. Next up were W.M. Haughton and Mrs R.R.W. Jackson who lost 6-1, 7-5. The third-round opponents were Ealing-born Olympic gold medal-winning Dorothea Lambert Chambers, who had also seven Ladies' Singles titles under her belt, and Irene Peacock from South Africa. They took the sisters to three sets but eventually succumbed 6-4, 3-6, 6-0. The semi-final against Dorothy Holman and Helen Aitchison was a walkover so the sisters got a free pass to the final. There they met French champion Suzanne Lenglen, one of the greatest Gallic sportswomen of all time, and American Elizabeth Ryan, the defending champions. The sisters could not compete and lost 6-0, 6-4.

DID YOU KNOW?

No more sisters made it through to a Wimbledon final until 2000, when Venus and Serena Williams, seeded number eight, beat Frenchwoman Julie Halard-Decugis and Japanese Ai Sugiyama in the final, 6-3, 6-2. The Williams sisters also won in 2002, 2008 and 2009 and triumphed in the US Open in 1999 and 2009.

FIRST

WIGHTMAN CUP

USA v Great Britain, Wightman Cup, West Side Tennis Club, One Tennis Place, Forest Hills, Queens, New York 11375, United States of America. Saturday, 11 – Monday, 13 August 1923

Hazel Hotchkiss was born at Healdsburg, California, and was a sickly child. It was suggested that she take up tennis to strengthen her body. Aged 25 she married George William Wightman of Boston, Massachusetts, and gave birth to five children. She dominated American women's tennis before the First World War and in her lifetime won 45 US titles – the last when she was 68. She came up with the idea of the Wightman Cup or the Ladies' International Tennis Challenge. It was first held in 1923 and Wightman played five times for America and was captain of the US team until 1948. The tournament consisted of five singles and two doubles matches. Wightman presented the cup in honour of her husband.

The first cup competition was due to start on Friday, 10 August 1923, but was postponed a day following the death of US President Warren G. Harding. No play took place on Sunday, 12 August so the competition ended on the Monday. The first Wightman Cup was won by the United States – winning all seven matches. The event opened the newly built stadium at Forest Hills, New York. Hazel Wightman played in the doubles competition alongside Eleanor Goss and they beat the British pair of Kathleen McKane and Phyllis Covell 10-8, 5-7, 6-4. In subsequent years, the Wightman Cup was played in even years in Great Britain and in odd years in America.

Wightman died at her home in the village of Chestnut Hill, Massachusetts, on 5 December 1974.

FIRST

PLAYER FROM OUTSIDE ANGLOSPHERE
TO WIN GENTLEMEN'S SINGLES AT WIMBLEDON

JEAN BOROTRA, GENTLEMEN'S SINGLES, THE CHAMPIONSHIPS, CHURCH ROAD, WIMBLEDON, SURREY SW, ENGLAND. SATURDAY, 5 JULY 1924

Until 1924, all the winners of the Gentlemen's Singles at Wimbledon had come from the Anglosphere. From 1924 onwards that would change. Indeed, whichever finalist won the title in that year would have been a first from outside the Anglosphere because Frenchman Jean Borotra beat his compatriot René Lacoste to take the title. The following year, the situation was reversed when Lacoste beat Borotra. Borotra returned to winning ways in 1926, beating the American Howard Kinsey but the finals in 1927, 1928 and 1929 were all-Gallic affairs. In 1927, Henri Cochet beat Borotra, in 1928, Lacoste beat Cochet and in 1929 Cochet returned to beat Borotra. Jacques Brugnon was **the only one of the Four Musketeers not to win a singles title at Wimbledon**.

FIRST

MAN TO WIN AUSTRALIAN CHAMPIONSHIPS
IN TWO CONSECUTIVE YEARS

James Anderson, Men's Singles, Australasian Championships, Warehouseman's Cricket Ground, St Kilda Road, Melbourne, Victoria 3000, Australia. January 1924; Men's Singles, Australian Championships, White City Stadium, Rushcutters Bay, Sydney, New South Wales 2021, Australia. January 1925

James Outram Anderson was born on 17 September 1894 at Enfield, Sydney and went to Camden Grammar School. In 1912, Anderson was the first interstate player to win the Victorian Schoolboys' Singles Championship. In 1919, he represented Australasia in the Davis Cup Challenge Round and with Gerald Patterson beat the British Isles in Sydney. Anderson again played for Australasia in 1922 and Australia in 1923 in the Challenge Rounds played in New York. He won the Australian Men's Singles in 1922, 1924 and 1925 and, with Norman Brookes, the Australian Men's Doubles in 1924, defeating Aussies Pat O'Hara-Wood and Gerald Patterson 6-2, 6-4, 6-3. The first two singles titles did not come with ease – Anderson needed five sets each time. All of his three championships were won by beating fellow Aussies – 1922 over Gerald Patterson 6-0, 3-6, 3-6, 6-3, 6-2, 1924 over Richard Schlesinger, 6-3, 6-4, 3-6, 5-7, 6-3 and 1925 over Patterson again, 11-9, 2-6, 6-2, 6-3.

Anderson's success was mainly restricted to his own country, although he won the Gentlemen's Doubles at Wimbledon with Randolph Lycett in 1922, beating Aussies O'Hara-Wood and Patterson 3-6, 7-9, 6-4, 6-3, 11-9. Nicknamed "The Greyhound", Anderson took a toy kangaroo mascot onto the court whenever he played. Rival Bill Tilden said of

Anderson that he was "tall, ungainly, almost awkward, taciturn, grim, unsmiling, yet interesting and to a great majority of all who see him fascinating ... [He] gives the impression of ruthlessness in play which is so often belied by his charming smile and generous acknowledgment of his opponent's good shots". In 1923, Anderson had a disagreement with the Lawn Tennis Association of Australia when it refused to make good his business losses that he had run up during his overseas tours, with the consequence he refused to represent Australia in 1924. In December 1926 Anderson turned professional and set himself up as a tennis coach in Sydney. Anderson died on 23 December 1973 at Gosford. In 2013 he was inducted in the International Tennis Hall of Fame.

ONLY

MEMBER OF THE BRITISH ROYAL FAMILY
TO PLAY AT WIMBLEDON

HRH THE DUKE OF YORK, GENTLEMEN'S DOUBLES, THE CHAMPIONSHIPS, CHURCH ROAD, WIMBLEDON, SURREY SW, ENGLAND. FRIDAY, 25 JUNE 1926

Albert Frederick Arthur George, Duke of York, known to the family as Bertie, was the second son of HM King George V and for much of his early life lived in the shadow of his glamorous elder brother, the Prince of Wales (later HM King Edward VIII, then HRH the Duke of Windsor). Bertie was a keen tennis player and with his friend and mentor Wing Commander Louis Greig (the grandfather of *Daily Mail* editor Geordie Greig) won the RAF Doubles Championship on 8 July 1920. In June 1926, they competed in the Gentlemen's Doubles at Wimbledon. Sensing a publicity coup, the authorities wanted their match to be played on Centre Court but the shy Bertie demurred and asked for one of the outer courts. A compromise was reached and the match was scheduled for Number Two Court. In the first round, the pair were drawn against former champions Arthur Gore, 58, and 52-year-old Herbert Roper Barrett. A witness recalled, "The crowd was in very close around the court ... The Duke of York was very nervous and couldn't play at all, at times lashing at the ball with his racquet. The crowd began muttering and someone made the well-meaning suggestion to the left-handed prince 'Try the other hand, sir.'" The prince and the equerry were knocked out in the first round 6-1, 6-3, 6-2. One of the ball boys at the match was Dan Maskell. After the match, Bertie told the tournament referee, Frank Burrow, that the Wimbledon standard was too high for him. He never played tennis in public again.

ONLY

MARRIED COUPLE TO WIN THE MIXED DOUBLES AT WIMBLEDON

LESLIE AND KITTY GODFREE, MIXED DOUBLES, THE CHAMPIONSHIPS, CHURCH ROAD, WIMBLEDON, SURREY SW, ENGLAND. SATURDAY, 3 JULY 1926

Leslie Godfree played in the Wimbledon Championships every year from 1920 until 1930, although he never got past the third round (which he reached in 1923). He played (and lost) in the first match on Centre Court when the new Church Road ground opened (see p.77). In 1923, he also won the Gentlemen's Doubles title with Randolph Lycett, beating the Spanish pair Manuel de Gomar and Edouard Flaquer 6-3, 6-4, 3-6, 6-3. Count de Gomar retired that year because of illness and died in January 1935, aged just 37.

In 1924, Godfree reached the finals of the Mixed Doubles (with Dorothy Shepherd-Barron) and lost to Kitty McKane and John Gilbert 6-3, 3-6, 6-3. In January 1926, Godfree married McKane and that summer she won the Ladies' Singles title at Wimbledon for the second time. In that same year, she and her husband became the only married couple to win the Mixed Doubles. In the first round, they beat Donald Stralem and Dorothy Hill 6-1, 6-0. Their second-round opponents proved slightly more troublesome, with the score being 6-2, 6-3. In the third round, they faced Briton Eden Petchell and the Swiss Charles Aeschlimann, who provided little opposition, going down 6-1, 6-3. Their opponents in the quarter-final were R.D.N. Pryce-Jones and Irene Maltby and the Godfrees won 6-4, 6-0. In the semi-final they met the

American pairing of Vinnie Richards and Elizabeth Ryan and won 7-5, 6-4. In the final they met two more Americans, Howard Kinsey and Mary Browne, both from California. Kinsey was playing in his third final and was tired, causing him to make several mistakes in the first set, which the Godfrees won 6-3. When Browne lost her serve in the seventh game of the second set, it appeared to be all over – until Leslie Godfree lost his. However, the Godfrees went on to win 6-4 and take the title. In 1927, the Godfrees again reached the final but comprehensively lost to Elizabeth Ryan and Frank Hunter 8-6, 6-0. Kitty Godfree was inducted into the International Tennis Hall of Fame in 1978. She died, aged 96, on 19 June 1992.

DID YOU KNOW?

Dorothy Shepherd-Barron's eldest son, John, is credited with inventing the first cash machine or ATM, which was opened at Barclays Bank in Enfield, Middlesex, on 27 June 1967 by the *On the Buses* actor Reg Varney. Dorothy Shepherd-Barron was killed in a car crash in Melbourn, Cambridgeshire on 20 February 1953.

FIRST

PROFESSIONAL TENNIS TOUR
UNITED STATES OF AMERICA/CANADA. SATURDAY, 9 OCTOBER 1926

From its inception, tennis had been a sport for amateurs, but the players began to agitate that they were making no money from their talents and, in 1926, America's first sports agent Charles C. Pyle – nicknamed Cash and Carry Pyle – organised the first professional tennis tour, around the United States of America and Canada. Its star attraction was Pyle's client Suzanne Lenglen – she was the only tennis player at the time who could attract a paying audience and Pyle offered her $50,000. He offered $25,000 to Mary K. Browne to play her. Lenglen won all 38 matches on the tour. Other players were Americans Vincent Richards ($35,000), Howard O. Kinsey ($20,000), and Harvey Snodgrass ($12,000) and Frenchman Paul Peret ($10,000). The tour began at Madison Square

Garden and was so successful that Pyle earned $80,000 himself and was able to give Lenglen a $25,000 bonus.

FIRST

WOMAN TO APPEAR AT WIMBLEDON WITHOUT STOCKINGS

Billie Tapscott, Ladies' Singles, The Championships, Church Road, Wimbledon, Surrey SW, England. Wednesday, 22 June 1927

Daphne Ruth – known as Billie – Tapscott was born at Kimberley, South Africa on 31 May 1903. In 1927, she achieved her best performance in a Grand Slam singles tournament when she reached the quarter-finals of the French Championships before losing to eventual winner Kea Bouman in straight sets. That year, she caused a sensation when she appeared on an outside court without stockings against the Frenchwoman Mlle G Cousin, who she beat 7-5, 6-4 in the second round. In the third round, Tapscott lost to Kitty Godfree 6-2, 10-8. Tapscott won the South African Championships Singles title in 1930, 1933, 1934 and 1938. Her brothers, Lionel and George, played Test cricket for South Africa. She died in 1970.

FIRST

DAVIS CUP WIN BY FRANCE

FIRST

DAVIS CUP ENTRANCE BY GREECE

FIRST

DAVIS CUP ENTRANCE BY YUGOSLAVIA

INTERNATIONAL LAWN TENNIS CHALLENGE, GERMANTOWN CRICKET CLUB, 411 WEST MANHEIM STREET, PHILADELPHIA, PENNSYLVANIA 19144, UNITED STATES OF AMERICA. THURSDAY, 8 - SATURDAY, 10 SEPTEMBER 1927

The 1927 International Lawn Tennis Challenge was the 22nd time what is now known as the Davis Cup was held. In all, 25 countries entered – 21 in the Europe Zone and four (Canada, Cuba, Japan and Mexico) in the America Zone. Greece and Yugoslavia entered for the first time while Germany returned to the fold for the first time since 1914. In the America Zone, Japan beat Mexico by four matches to one and Canada bested Cuba 3-2. In the final, held in August 1927, Japan beat Canada 3-2. With more countries, the Europe Zone matches began in April 1927. In the second round, Greece lost 4-1 to Czechoslovakia and India beat Yugoslavia 3-0. Like Greece and Yugoslavia, Germany received a bye in the first round. In the second round, they achieved a 5-0 whitewash over Portugal but were beaten 4-1 by South Africa in the third round. With the Four Musketeers representing France, they beat Denmark 3-0 in the final, held on clay in Copenhagen on 21–22 July 1927. On 25–27 August 1927 at the Longwood Cricket Club, Boston, Massachusetts, United States, France defeated Japan 3-0 in the Inter-Zonal play-off. In the final at the Germantown Cricket Club in Philadelphia, Pennsylvania, the Four Musketeers proved too much for the Americans, despite the presence of the Bills – Tilden and Johnston. René Lacoste beat Bill Johnston in straight sets, then Bill Tilden got the better of Henri Cochet in four sets before Tilden and Frank Hunter beat Jean Borotra and Jacques Brugnon in five sets in the doubles match. Lacoste beat Tilden in four sets and Cochet beat Johnston, also in four sets, to wrap up victory for France after six consecutive United States' wins. That win gave the French the right to host the 1928 Davis Cup. To build a fitting stadium, the French Tennis Association bought land on the western edge of Paris. The new venue was named after French war hero, Roland Garros.

DID YOU KNOW?

Roland Garros was born at Saint-Denis de la Réunion on 6 October 1888 and founded his own business – a car dealership not far from the Arc de Triomphe – when he was 21. In August 1909, he went to an air show in the Champagne region and became obsessed with aeroplanes. He bought a plane and taught himself how to fly before getting his pilot's licence. On 6 September 1911 he broke an altitude record, reaching a little under 13,000 feet. On 23 September 1913 he flew from Saint-Raphaël on the French Riviera to Bizerte in Tunisia in his Morane-Saulnier monoplane – the first flight across the Mediterranean. Garros landed in Tunisia at 1.40pm after flying 485 miles in just under eight hours. During the First World War, he developed the first on-board machine gun that fired through the propeller. In April 1915, his plane was hit and he was captured, spending the next three years in a prisoner of war camp. Having escaped, he returned to flying but was shot down and killed on 5 October 1918 over the Ardennes. Oddly, although a keen sportsman, Garros was not much of a tennis fan; he preferred football, rugby and cycling. The new stadium was opened on 18 May 1928 and a month later, the French Championships were held there for the first time and the name Roland Garros was adopted. On 27 July 1928, the Davis Cup final took place.

FIRST

SEEDING IN US NATIONAL CHAMPIONSHIPS

US NATIONAL CHAMPIONSHIPS, WEST SIDE TENNIS CLUB, ONE TENNIS PLACE, FOREST HILLS, QUEENS, NEW YORK 11375 UNITED STATES OF AMERICA. MONDAY, 22 AUGUST – SATURDAY, 17 SEPTEMBER 1927

The 1927 US National Championships competition – the 47th – was the first in which players were seeded to prevent the best players playing each other in the early rounds. The women's tournament began on 22 August and finished eight days later while the men's got underway on 12 September and lasted until 17 September. On this occasion, there were two sets of seeds in the men's competition – one for the Americans and one for the foreign players.

DID YOU KNOW?

The Americans were seeded thus (with their final performance in brackets):

1 Bill Tilden (finalist)
2 Bill Johnston (semi-finalist)
3 Manuel Alonso (quarter-finalist; despite being Spanish he lived in America making him eligible for an American seeding)
4 Frank Hunter (semi-finalist)
5 George Lott (first round)
6 Richard Norris Williams (first round)
7 Lewis White (third round)
8 John Doeg (third round)

The foreign players were seeded thus:
1 René Lacoste (winner)
2 Henri Cochet (third round)
3 Jean Borotra (quarter-finalist)
4 Jacques Brugnon (quarter-finalist)
5 Jean Washer (third round)
6 Jack Wright (third round)
7 Yoshiro Ohta (second round)
8 Ryuki Miki (first round)

The seeding worked as the top two seeds in each group reached the final and Lacoste ran out the winner 11-9, 6-3, 11-9. Helen Wills was the top seeded woman and she went on to win the title, beating the number three seed Betty Nuthall from Britain 6-1, 6-4.

ONLY

BRITISH PLAYER TO BEAT
BILL TILDEN

Eric Peters v Bill Tilden, Carlton Tournament, Cannes, France. February 1930

Eric Peters, 26, beat Bill Tilden, 37, in the second round of the Carlton Tournament at Cannes, France. Peters was victorious 9-7, 8-6.

ONLY
GENTLEMEN'S SINGLES PLAYER AT
WIMBLEDON WHO WON WITHOUT HITTING A FINAL STROKE

Sidney Wood, Gentlemen's Singles final, The Championships, Church Road, Wimbledon, Surrey SW, England. Saturday, 4 July 1931

Tennis fans were looking forward to the 1931 Gentlemen's Singles competition at Wimbledon. Some top tennis talent had arrived in Surrey to battle it out. Two of the Four Musketeers from France – Jean Borotra and Henri Cochet – were seeded numbers one and two. Fred Perry and Bunny Austin were five and six and the Japanese Jiro Sato was eighth seed. At number three and number seven were, respectively, the Americans Frank Shields and Sidney Wood. There was disappointment when Henri Cochet was knocked out in the first round in straight sets by the Briton Nigel Sharpe 6-1, 6-3, 6-2, but the other seeds progressed in the tournament, gradually falling. Sato and Austin went out in the quarter-finals and Borotra and Perry reached the semi-finals, losing to Shields and Wood respectively. (Sidney Wood, at 19, was the youngest finalist of the 20th century until his record was usurped by Boris Becker in 1985.)

The Americans in Surrey and around the world were looking forward to an all-American, Fourth of July Wimbledon final. Towards the end of his 7-5, 3-6, 6-4, 6-4 semi-final win over the Frenchman, Shields had twisted his ankle, but after a 12-minute courtside massage, he had upheld the honour of his country. It promised to be a cracking final – until the American Davis Cup captain Gene Dixon stuck his oar in the water and announced the ankle was too painful and Shields would not be able to compete in the final against Wood. The title was awarded to Wood without a ball being served in anger, thanks to Shields's "injury".

The real reason was that a week after Wimbledon, the United States had a Davis Cup match that they were desperate to win. The Davis Cup match came around and the seemingly crocked Shields beat Fred Perry 10-8, 6-4, 6-2. However, cheats never prosper, and Britain won the tie three games to two. Perry told American George Lott, "Your boys seemed very overconfident and they are not really that good, you know." The United States would have to wait until 1937 to reclaim the trophy. Wood later commented, "Frank wanted to play me and it was an insult to Wimbledon and the public that he didn't. But it gives you an idea of the importance of the Davis Cup then, and the USLTA's tight control of American amateurs. Can you imagine a player today abandoning a Wimbledon final to save himself for the Davis Cup? But, as amateurs, we had no say."

DID YOU KNOW?

As well as being the only man to surrender a Wimbledon final without hitting a ball, Francis Xavier Alexander "Frank" Shields (1909–1975) had another claim to fame. By his second wife, he had two children – Frank Junior (1941–2003) and Marina (b. 1943). In 1964, Frank Junior married Teri Schmon (1933–2012) and on 31 May 1965, Teri gave birth to a baby who would grow up to be the actress Brooke Shields and, in 1997, marry tennis champion Andre Agassi, only to divorce in 1999.

FIRST

MAN TO WIN AUSTRALIAN CHAMPIONSHIPS THREE CONSECUTIVE YEARS

Jack Crawford, Men's Singles, Australian Championships, White City Stadium, Rushcutters Bay, Sydney, New South Wales 2021, Australia. Monday, 9 March 1931; Men's Singles, Australian Championships, Memorial Drive Tennis Club, 1626 War Memorial Drive, North Adelaide, South Australia 5006, Australia. Saturday, 13 February 1932; Men's Singles, Australian Championships, Kooyong Lawn Tennis Club, 489 Glenferrie Road, Kooyong, Victoria 3144, Australia. Tuesday, 31 January 1933

John Herbert Crawford was born on 21 March 1908 at Albury, New South Wales, the fifth of six children of a farmer. His father, John McNeill Crawford, fashioned a court for all the children to play on at home. Young Jack was by far the best and represented the local town in competitions. In 1920, the Crawfords moved to Sydney after a drought forced them to sell the farm but Jack persisted with his tennis. He won the Australian junior championships every year from 1926 to 1929. He represented Australia in Davis Cup ties in 1928, 1930, and from 1932 to 1937, and was a member of the 1939 winning team although he did not play. In 1929, he and wife, Marjorie Cox, who he would marry on 28 February 1930, began the first of five consecutive appearances in the Mixed Doubles finals at the Australian Championships. Although seeded number one, they lost to the fourth-seeded Daphne Akhurst and Gar Moon 6-0, 7-5 in the final. In 1930, they were runners-up again. Two couples who would both end up marrying their partner contested the final. Nell Hall and Harry Hopman bested Marjorie Cox and Jack Crawford 11-9, 3-6, 6-3 to win the Mixed Doubles title. In 1931, seeded number one, he won the Australian Championships for the first time beating the number two seed Harry Hopman 6-4, 6-2, 2-6, 6-1. With wife, Marjorie, Crawford was seeded number one in the Mixed Doubles. They beat the unseeded Emily Hood Westacott and Aubrey Willard 7-5, 6-4 to take the title. The Crawfords retained their title in 1932 beating Meryl O'Hara Wood and Jiro Sato 6-8, 8-6, 6-3 in the final. That year, Crawford also retained his singles title in a repeat of the 1931 final. Crawford, seeded number one, beat Hopman, downgraded to the number four seed, over five sets 4-6, 6-3, 3-6, 6-3, 6-1. The next year – 1933 – was Crawford's year. He won the Australian and French Mixed Doubles (with Briton Peggy Scriven) championships and the Australian (Crawford was the number two seed and beat the number seven seed Keith Gledhill 2-6, 7-5, 6-3, 6-2), French (beating the first-seeded, and reigning champion, Henri Cochet 8-6, 6-1, 6-3), and Wimbledon (he beat the number one seed and the defending champion Ellsworth Vines 4-6, 11-9, 6-2, 2-6, 6-4) singles titles, failing to become the first to win the Grand Slam when beaten in five sets by Fred Perry in the United

States final losing 3-6, 13-11, 6-4, 0-6, 1-6. An asthmatic, Crawford found it difficult to play lengthy matches. He was leading Perry by two sets to one when his strength began to wane. He was also known for taking a shot of whisky mixed with sugar between sets if he found the match becoming tense and his breathing was becoming laboured. On that muggy afternoon in Forest Hills, Crawford was said to have downed two or three doses of his whisky and sugar mix, but there are various versions of what the Australian actually drank. "Jack Crawford was one of the most popular champions who ever appeared at Wimbledon," wrote Duncan Macaulay, the club secretary. "Although he was only 25 when he won the title, he always seemed much older. Perhaps it was the effect of his hairstyle, the sleeves of his cricket shirt buttoned at the wrist and, most of all, the old-fashioned square-headed racquet with which he always played. In a long match, he liked to have a pot of tea, complete with milk and sugar, and reserves of hot water by the umpire's chair, instead of the iced beverages and other revivers favoured by the moderns." In their fifth consecutive appearance in the Mixed Doubles final in 1933, Marjorie and Jack Crawford successfully defended their title for the third year in a row by beating Midge Van Ryn and Ellsworth Vines 3-6, 7-5, 13-11. Known as "Gentleman Jack", 6ft Crawford was renowned for his politeness on court. He played in long flannel trousers and a long-sleeved shirt, which was buttoned at the wrist. He never wore shorts and claimed that the long, Viyella sleeves soaked up any sweat and kept his hands dry. Only thirteen players in tennis history have completed a three-quarter slam in singles competition and Crawford was the first, in 1933. Only fifteen players in tennis history have completed a three-quarter slam in doubles competition and Crawford was the third to reach that milestone in 1935. He was inducted into the International Tennis Hall of Fame in 1979. He died on 10 September 1991 at Cessnock. He was inducted into the Australian Tennis Hall of Fame in 1997.

———•❈•———

FIRST
MAN TO WEAR SHORTS AT WIMBLEDON
Bunny Austin, Gentlemen's Singles, The Championships, Church Road, Wimbledon, Surrey SW, England. Monday, 26 June 1933

Long, heavy, white flannel trousers for men and ankle-length dresses for women was the accepted dress code at Wimbledon. That all changed in 1933 when the Englishman Bunny Austin took to the Wimbledon court in shorts. On 5 September 1932, when Austin and Fred Perry were playing in America, Austin wore shorts for the first time on court in his four-set victory over Berkeley Bell in the first round of the US Championships at Forest Hills. John Kieran of the *New York Times* wrote, "Austin came dressed for the occasion. He was practically in running costume." Austin recalled, "Fred Perry and I were playing in the doubles at Longwood [in Brookline, Massachusetts], and it was terribly hot. I came off the court in those sweat-soaked trousers feeling I was carrying an awful lot of unnecessary weight below my knees. I wasn't very big. I'd been a football player in school – Repton and Cambridge – and, of course, we wore shorts. Best thing for running. Why not for tennis? We went to New York for the singles at Forest Hills, and I bought a pair and wore them. I got a lot of kidding, but the wisdom of it was apparent. The next year, I introduced them at Wimbledon. I expected a fuss there, but there was none. Slowly, others followed. I don't know why we put up with long flannel trousers for so long." Kieran wrote in the *New York Times*, "With his white linen hat and his flannel shorts, the little English player looked like an A.A. Milne production."

At Wimbledon, King George V and Queen Mary accepted the change without comment, and soon other men, and then women, led by the American Helen Hull Jacobs, started wearing shorts too. Austin was the number four seed in 1933. He made it to the quarter-finals before losing to the Japanese Jiro Sato 5-7, 3-6, 6-2, 6-2, 2-6. In 1932, Sato had made headlines worldwide when he defeated the defending Wimbledon champion Sidney Wood at the quarter-final stage before losing to Austin in the semi-final.

FIRST

JAPANESE PLAYERS TO REACH A WIMBLEDON FINAL

JIRO SATO AND RYOSUKE NUNOI, GENTLEMEN'S DOUBLES, THE CHAMPIONSHIPS, CHURCH ROAD, WIMBLEDON, SURREY SW, ENGLAND. SATURDAY, 8 JULY 1933

Jiro Sato and Ryosuke Nunoi were unseeded at the Gentlemen's Doubles at Wimbledon in 1933. In the first round they beat Hungarian Béla von Kehrling and his Spanish partner Enrique Maier 6-3, 6-4, 6-4. Their second round opponents, the South African pair Jack Condon and Colin Robbins, proved slightly tougher to beat, 6-1, 5-7, 6-1, 6-2. In the third round, the British pair of Bill Latham and George Gibbs were no match for the Japanese duo, who triumphed 6-3, 6-1, 6-1. In the quarter-final they beat the English number three seeds Fred Perry and Pat Hughes in five sets 5-7, 6-3, 6-4, 1-6, 6-3. Their semi-final opponents were the Germans, Gottfried von Cramm and Eberhard Nourney. The Japanese pair won 7-5, 3-6, 6-4, 6-1. They could not maintain their success and lost in the final to the number one seeds Jean Borotra and Jacques Brugnon, despite winning the first set 6-4. The Musketeers proved why they were reigning champions, winning the remaining three sets 6-3, 6-3, 7-5. In August 1933, Nunoi and Sato won the doubles title at the German Championships in Hamburg.

DID YOU KNOW?

Both of the Japanese players came to tragic ends. Jiro Sato was born in Japan on 5 January 1908 and was ranked number three in the world in 1933. The pressure from his country to do well became intolerable for Sato. On 4 April 1934, he was aboard NYK *Hakone Maru*, crossing the Strait of Malacca, bound for Europe for a second round Davis Cup match against Australia. Sato said he had pains in his stomach and stayed in his cabin. When the ship docked in Singapore, he went to see a doctor who could find nothing wrong and believed his pains were psychosomatic and caused by the stress he felt. Sato was convinced his illness would cause Japan to lose and he and the country would be shamed. He did not wish to proceed with the journey. That night, the Japanese consul to Singapore hosted a banquet for the country's Davis Cup team. The consul and his team-mates encouraged Sato to go to Europe. Later, a telegram was received from the Japanese Lawn Tennis Association ordering Sato to participate.

The next day, he ate dinner in his cabin at 8.30pm. Three hours later, before reaching Penang, his team-mate Jiro Yamagishi went to find him but the cabin was empty. Instead, he found two letters. One was addressed to his team-mates, apologising for letting them down. He explained that he would not be good enough to help them win and begged their forgiveness. He urged them to do their best in the match. The other letter was to the ship's captain apologising for any inconvenience caused. The ship stayed in situ for seven hours as a search was launched for the missing tennis player. The search revealed that iron davit-winding handles and a training skip-rope were missing, leading to the belief that Sato had used them to tie weights to his body so he would drown. The ship then sent out a message that "Japan's finest tennis player and national hero was believed to have committed suicide by throwing himself overboard." The next day, his team-mates held a memorial service on the deck of the ship. Fred Perry commented that Sato was "one of the cheeriest men he had ever known". Bunny Austin said, "He had a great sense of humour … He always gave the impression that he would be the last man on earth to come to such an end." His fiancée said, "I believe Jiro committed suicide solely from a sense of responsibility after he had acceded to the tennis association's urgings to proceed to Europe, even when he wanted to return from Singapore. To the end of my life I shall regret that it was the order of the Japanese Lawn Tennis Association that resulted in his death. Jiro was a man of honour and he played every time for the honour of Japan." He was 26 years old.

Ryosuke Nunoi was born into a wealthy family in Kobe on 18 January 1909. He was the youngest player in the Japanese team that toured Australia in 1932. That year, he and Sato were quarter-finalists in the Australian Championships Singles. The pair remained the only of their countrymen to reach the quarter-finals at the championships until 2012, when Kei Nishikori achieved that feat. In 1933, Nunoi appeared in Davis Cup matches against Hungary,

Ireland, Germany and Australia. At the French Championships that year he was the number 12 seed and reached the third round, losing to Marcel Bernard. He was the number ten seed in the 1933 US National Championships and reached the fourth round. When the Second World War broke out, he became a paymaster captain with the Imperial Japanese Army. On 21 July 1945, aged 36, he committed suicide.

FIRST

NON-AUSTRALIAN TO WIN
AUSTRALIAN CHAMPIONSHIPS WOMEN'S SINGLES

DOROTHY ROUND, WOMEN'S SINGLES, AUSTRALIAN OPEN, KOOYONG LAWN TENNIS CLUB, 489 GLENFERRIE ROAD, KOOYONG, VICTORIA 3144, AUSTRALIA. JANUARY 1935

Beginning in 1922 as the Australasian Championships, it became the Australian Championships in 1927. The competition was won by Australians until 1935, when Briton Dorothy Round, the number one seed, beat fellow Briton and number four seed Nancy Lyle 1-6, 6-1, 6-3.

LAST

ENGLISHMAN TO WIN
WIMBLEDON GENTLEMEN'S SINGLES

LAST

ENGLISHMAN TO WIN
WIMBLEDON GENTLEMEN'S SINGLES
THREE TIMES IN A ROW

Fred Perry, Gentlemen's Singles, The Championships, Church Road, Wimbledon, Surrey SW, England. Friday, 6 July 1934; Gentlemen's Singles, The Championships, Church Road, Wimbledon, Surrey SW, England. Friday, 5 July 1935; Gentlemen's Singles, The Championships, Church Road, Wimbledon, Surrey SW, England. Friday, 3 July 1936

Fred Perry was born on 18 May 1909 at 33 Carrington Road, Stockport but moved to Brentham Garden Suburb in Ealing, west London when he was 11. His father, Samuel, was a cotton spinner who, in 1923, was elected Labour and Co-operative Party MP for Kettering. He lost the seat the following year, regained it in 1929 but held it for only two more years. (In 1940, John Profumo was elected for the constituency in a by-election but lost it in the Labour landslide of 1945.) In 1928, Fred Perry won his first international honours, picking up a bronze medal in the Men's Doubles, Mixed Doubles and team event at the Table Tennis World Championships in Stockholm. In January 1929 in Budapest, he added to his medal tally, taking a bronze in the Doubles and team competitions and a gold in the Men's Singles. Perry began playing tennis on public courts in Ealing, while he was working for the sporting goods manufacturers Spaldings. He first appeared at Wimbledon in the 1929 Championships but was knocked out in the third round by fellow Briton John Oliff, a former public schoolboy. The next year, Spaldings refused Perry the time off to play in the British Hard Court Championships. His father stepped in and offered to support him for a year while he attempted to get to the top in the amateur sport. It cost Sam Perry about £10 (£625 at 2020 values) a week in entrance fees, fares and hotel expenses. Mr Perry also promised Fred £100 (£6,250, 2020) if he did not drink alcohol before his 21st birthday. In May 1930, Perry collected the money. In 1931, he was chosen for the Davis Cup. Britain lost the final to France by three matches to two. Two years later, Great Britain defeated France in Paris in the final 3-2, with Perry taking the deciding rubber. More than 10,000 people turned up at Victoria Station to welcome the returning heroes and King George V sent a telegram of congratulations. The team of Bunny Austin, Pat Hughes, Harry Lee, and Perry retained the Davis Cup for the next three years, but the British would not win it again until 2015.

Perry won Wimbledon for the first time in 1934 and held the title for two years running after that. In 1934, he was the number two seed. In the first round, he beat fellow Briton Raymond Tuckey 6-2, 6-2, 5-7, 6-0 before overcoming American R. Norris Williams 6-2, 6-2, 6-0. His third-round opponent was the Czechoslovakian Roderich Menzel who he beat 0-6, 6-3, 5-7, 6-4, 6-2. The Australian Adrian Quist provided little competition in the fourth round, losing 6-2, 6-3, 6-4. The quarter and semi-final opponents were both American. George Lott lost 6-4, 2-6, 7-5, 10-8 and Sidney Wood went down 6-3, 3-6, 7-5, 5-7, 6-3. In the final, Perry met the defending champion, Australian Jack Crawford. Perry had beaten Crawford in five sets to take the US Championships and in three sets to take the Australian title and this time he won in straight sets 6-3, 6-0, 7-5. At one stage Crawford was up 5-4 in the third set but "Perry just opened the throttle a little wider". The match – and championship – was Perry's on a double fault. Crawford served what he thought was an ace only for a linesman to foot-fault him. On his second serve he hit the net to give the title to the Englishman. Crawford bowed sarcastically to the linesman while Perry did a cartwheel before leaping the net to shake hands with his opponent. The match took an hour and ten minutes to complete.

He retained his title in 1935, beating Canadian Marcel Rainville 6-1, 6-1, 6-3 in round one. He saw off Americans Wilmer Hines 6-1, 7-5, 6-3 and John Van Ryn 4-6, 6-1, 6-3, 10-8 in the second and third rounds respectively. In the fourth round he beat Josip Palada from the Kingdom of Yugoslavia 6-2, 6-2, 0-6, 6-2. In the quarter-final he met Menzel, the number seven seed, looking for revenge for his third-round defeat the previous year. He did not get it as, after a hesitant start, Perry won 9-7, 6-1, 6-1. His opponent in the semi-final was the man he had beaten in the 1934 final, Crawford, the number three seed. The match was won by Perry 6-2, 3-6, 6-4, 6-4. In the final, he played the German number two seed Gottfried von Cramm and won 6-2, 6-4, 6-4.

In 1936, he was seeded number one and beat second seed von Cramm 6-1, 6-1, 6-0 in the final, which lasted just 40 minutes. It was the quickest final in the 20th century and the second shortest of all time. Talking to the Wimbledon masseur, Perry gleaned that von Cramm had been suffering from a groin strain and found it hard to move wide on a forehand. Perry also had spies at the Savoy where von Cramm was staying, so he knew his routine intimately. To maintain his own fitness, Perry trained with Arsenal.

DID YOU KNOW?

Fred Perry was not accepted by the Wimbledon establishment although the public loved him. In those days, there was no official presentation of a trophy to the winner. The finalists shook hands and then retired to the dressing room. In 1934, after he won his first title, Perry got into the bath for a well-deserved soak. As he lay there, "the proudest bloke in a bathtub anywhere in England", he heard Wimbledon committee member Brame Hillyard tell the beaten finalist Jack Crawford that "this was one day when the best man didn't win". He even gave a bottle of champagne to Crawford. Perry leapt out of the tub: "I don't think I've ever been so angry in all my life." All winners receive an All England Club member's tie – Perry's was left on a dressing room chair for him to collect. Perry was next due to play in the Davis Cup but refused until he got an apology. It took several days to arrive.

FIRST
PLAYER TO WIN A CAREER GRAND SLAM

FRED PERRY, MEN'S SINGLES, US CHAMPIONSHIPS, WEST SIDE TENNIS CLUB, ONE TENNIS PLACE, FOREST HILLS, QUEENS, NEW YORK 11375, UNITED STATES OF AMERICA. SUNDAY, 10 SEPTEMBER 1933; MEN'S SINGLES, AUSTRALIAN CHAMPIONSHIPS, WHITE CITY STADIUM, RUSHCUTTERS BAY, SYDNEY, NEW SOUTH WALES 2021, AUSTRALIA. SATURDAY, 27 JANUARY 1934; GENTLEMEN'S SINGLES, THE CHAMPIONSHIPS, CHURCH ROAD, WIMBLEDON, SURREY SW, ENGLAND. FRIDAY, 6 JULY 1934; MEN'S SINGLES, FRENCH CHAMPIONSHIPS, STADE ROLAND-GARROS, 2 AVENUE GORDON BENNETT, 75016 PARIS, FRANCE. SATURDAY, 1 JUNE 1935

Fred Perry was the first player to win a career Grand Slam, winning all four singles titles, although not holding the titles at the same time. On 10 September 1933, he triumphed at the US Championships, preventing Jack Crawford from becoming the first man to complete the Grand Slam. Crawford had already won the Australian Championships, French Championships and Wimbledon. He did not want to compete in the American tournament because he had spent five months on the road and was suffering from insomnia, exhaustion and asthma, but the Lawn Tennis Association of Australia forced Crawford to play because it had been promised $1,500 by the US Lawn Tennis Association if he did. Crawford and Perry were the number one and two seeds in the foreign list. Crawford nearly achieved the Slam, as he was two sets to one up at one stage but only won one game out of the last dozen, losing 6-3, 11-13, 4-6, 6-0, 6-1. Four months later, Crawford and Perry were again the number one and two seeds in the Australian Championships. Perry won, beating Crawford 6-3, 7-5, 6-1. Perry was the number one seed at the French Championships in 1934 but was knocked out in the quarter-final. He lost to the Italian Giorgio de Stefani, the number eight seed, 2-6, 6-1, 7-9, 2-6. Jack Crawford reached the final but lost to the German Gottfried von Cramm.

At Wimbledon later that year, Crawford was again seeded number one while Perry was second. Perry managed to take the title. In the French Championships, von Cramm was seeded one and Perry two. The Englishman joined the competition in the second round and beat Monegasque Vladimir Landau 3-6, 6-4, 6-3, 6-2. In the next round, he beat the Spaniard Enrique Maier 6-2, 6-4, 6-2. In the fourth round, he overcame the Australian Don Turnbull, the number 15 seed, 6-3, 6-3, 6-3. Moving into the quarter-final, Perry played Christian Boussus of France, the number 11 seed, and the Englishman won 6-1, 6-0, 6-4. In the semi-final, Perry met his nemesis Crawford, who was seeded number three. Perry won 6-3, 8-6, 6-3. In the other semi-final, von Cramm beat Englishman Bunny Austin in five sets – 6-2, 5-7, 6-1, 5-7, 6-0. The German took Perry to four sets in the final but eventually lost 3-6, 6-3, 1-6, 3-6. Perry achieved the milestone when he was 26 and remains **the only British player to achieve the career Grand Slam**. Perry later confessed, "I had never previously seemed able to string good tennis together for long enough on the slow clay of Roland-Garros Stadium, but this time it worked and I became the first Englishman to capture the French title."

FIRST

PROFESSIONAL MATCH PLAYED BY
FRED PERRY

Fred Perry v Ellsworth Vines, Madison Square Garden, 2 Pennsylvania Plaza, New York, NY10121 United States of America. Thursday, 7 January 1937

Having spent three years as the world's number one amateur, Fred Perry took the decision to turn professional in late 1936. The tennis establishment had never really welcomed what they saw as a maverick, and they turned their backs on Perry. He was stripped of membership of all the clubs where he had played, including the All England Club. Wimbledon did not welcome him back until 1949. His first match as a pro was against the American Ellsworth Vines and Perry won in four sets. More than 18,000 people attended Madison Square Garden that night and the gate receipts were $52,000. In 1937 they began a regular one-on-one competition – Perry won 29 matches and Vines 32. Then they played in Britain where Perry won six to Vines's three – leaving them tied at 35 wins each. The next year, Vines won 49 matches to Perry's 35. In a match in El Paso, Texas, Perry played a joke on his friend. He bribed the groundsman to make the service line three inches shorter resulting in Vines serving fault after fault. Perry did not confess to his misdemeanour until 1977, during the Wimbledon centenary celebrations. In July 1937, an England v America pro-celebrity tennis doubles match was arranged. It featured Perry and Charlie Chaplin playing against Groucho Marx and Vines, to celebrate the opening of the new clubhouse at the Beverly Hills Tennis Club. Perry and Vines owned a part of the club which had just six courts and 125 members. To join you had to earn at least $1,500 a week.

Among the members were Errol Flynn, David Niven, the Marx brothers, Benny Goodman and Norma Shearer. Perry and Vines maintained an interest in the club until the 1950s.

FIRST

TELEVISED WIMBLEDON CHAMPIONSHIP
The Championships, Church Road, Wimbledon, Surrey SW, England. Monday, 21 June 1937

The BBC broadcast 25 minutes of the first-round match between 6ft 7in Irishman George Lyttleton Rogers and Bunny Austin to between 1,500 and 2,000 homes in London. Austin lost the first set 6-3 and was 5-3 down in the second when he put on a lucky blue jockey cap and went on to win the set 8-6. He won the next two 6-1, 6-2 to take the match. The next day the *Daily Telegraph* said the coverage was excellent and "even the passage of the marks of the lawnmowers were distinctly visible". The first colour television broadcast of Wimbledon was on BBC Two at 2pm on 1 July 1967, the first Saturday of The Championships. The programme lasted four hours and was hosted by David Vine (1935–2009) with commentary from Keith Fordyce (1928–2011), better known as a radio disc jockey. The first match broadcast in colour was the fourth-round tie between South African Cliff Drysdale and Briton Roger Taylor and was played on the Centre Court. Taylor won 3-6, 11-9, 6-4, 4-6, 6-4.

The first tennis tournament to be broadcast on television in America was the Eastern Grass Court championship, which began on 9 August 1939 at the Westchester Country Club, Rye, New York. Station W2XBS used a telescopic lens to make sure important points were seen by its viewers. **The first colour tennis broadcast on television in America** was on 26 August 1955 when WNBT-TV showed the Davis Cup match between the United States and Australia which was held at the West Side Tennis Club, Forest Hills.

FIRST
MAN TO WIN A GRAND SLAM

ONLY

AMERICAN MAN TO WIN A
GRAND SLAM

Don Budge, v John Bromwich, Men's Singles, Australian
Championships Memorial Drive Tennis Club, 1626 War
Memorial Drive, North Adelaide, South Australia 5006,
Australia; Saturday, 29 January 1938; v Roderich Menzel,
Men's Singles, French Championships, Stade Roland-
Garros, 2 Avenue Gordon Bennett, 75016 Paris, France.
Saturday, 11 June 1938; v Bunny Austin, Gentlemen's
Singles, The Championships, Church Road, Wimbledon,
Surrey SW, England. Friday, 1 July 1938; v Gene Mako,
Men's Singles, United States Lawn Tennis Association
National Championships, West Side Tennis Club, One
Tennis Place, Forest Hills, Queens, New York 11375
United States of America. Saturday, 24 September 1938

American John Donald Budge was born in Oakland, California on 13
June 1915, the son of Jack Budge, a Scottish footballer who emigrated
to America. Like many athletes, he participated in a number of sports
before settling for one – in Budge's case tennis, but that was initially only
to please his elder brother Lloyd. From the age of 11 to 15, Budge did not
go near a tennis court, but, in June 1930, Lloyd chided his brother into
entering the California State Boys' Championship and he won through
to the final wearing corduroy trousers. In the final, he wore pristine
white slacks in which he beat Paul Newton 6-0, 6-4 – winning the first
competition he entered. On 2 July 1937, Budge won the Gentlemen's
Singles at Wimbledon for the first time, beating the German Gottfried
von Cramm in the final 6-3, 6-4, 6-2. Englishman Fred Perry had won
in 1936 but having turned professional was not eligible to enter the
competition. In January, Budge was the number one seed in the 1938

Australian Championships. In the second round, he saw off American Les Hancock in straight sets, 6-2, 6-3, 6-4. His next round opponent, Australian Harold Whillans, provided less of a battle as Budge won 6-1, 6-0, 6-1. In the quarter-final Budge came up against Australian Len Schwarz and won 6-4, 6-3, 10-8. In the semi-final he met Australian Adrian Quist, the number five seed. Budge won 6-4, 6-2, 8-6. In the final he came across fourth-seeded John Bromwich, his fifth Australian opponent. Budge won in straight sets 6-4, 6-2, 6-1 in under an hour before 6,500 spectators. (Quist and Bromwich would combine to win the Men's Doubles title.)

Next up was the French Championships which began on 2 June at the Stade Roland-Garros in Paris. It was **the only time Don Budge played in the French Championships**. He began his fight to win with a 6-1, 6-2, 6-4 win over the Frenchman Antoine Gentien. The third-round opponent was Ghaus Mohammad from India, who took Budge to four sets 6-1, 6-1, 5-7, 6-0. Franjo Kukuljević from Yugoslavia was a worthy opponent in the fourth round, taking Budge to five sets and coming back from two sets to love down. The American eventually won 6-2, 8-6, 2-6, 1-6, 6-1. In the quarter-final Budge beat Frenchman Bernard Destremau 6-4, 6-3, 6-4. His semi-final opponent was another Yugoslavian, Josip Palada, who went down 6-2, 6-3, 6-3. In the final, two days before his 23rd birthday, 6ft 1in Budge played 6ft 4in Czechoslovakian Roderich Menzel, the number three seed. Budge disposed of the Czechoslovakian 6-3, 6-2, 6-4 in under an hour. The triumph was even more impressive as Budge had suffered from diarrhoea during the tournament.

Less than a fortnight later, Budge was in England for the 58th Wimbledon Championships where he was again seeded number one. In the first round he was drawn to play Londoner Kenneth Gandar-Dower and won 6-2, 6-3, 6-3. In the second round he met Henry Billington (the grandfather of Tim Henman) and powered through 7-5, 6-1, 6-1. His third-round opponent was George Lyttleton Rogers and Budge won 6-0, 7-5, 6-1. The fourth-round match was played against Ronnie Shayes from Britain and Budge won 6-3, 6-4, 6-1. In the quarter-finals he played František Cejnar from Czechoslovakia and outplayed him 6-3, 6-0, 7-5. Yugoslavian Franjo Punčec played Budge in the semi-final but the American was too powerful for the Yugoslav and won 6-2, 6-1, 6-4. In the final he was up against the British number two seed Bunny Austin. The Briton proved no match for the powerful Budge, who retained his Wimbledon title, winning easily 6-1, 6-0, 6-3 and not losing a set en route to the title. Bunny Austin's appearance in the final was the last time a Briton appeared until Sir Andy Murray's defeat by Roger Federer in 2012.

To complete the Grand Slam, Budge had to win the fourth and final major – the US Championships. The 58th US Championships were due to take place from Thursday, 8 September until Saturday, 17 September. However, the bad weather caused by the New England hurricane meant the competition did not actually finish until a week later. In his first match, the redheaded Budge easily saw off fellow American Welby Van Horn 6-0, 6-0, 6-1. The third-round match was against another American, Bob Kamrath, and Budge won 6-3, 7-5, 9-7. In the fourth round, Budge beat Englishman Charles Hare 6-3, 6-4, 6-0 to progress to a quarter-final tie against Harry Hopman from Australia. Budge saw him off 6-3, 6-1, 6-3. His semi-final opponent was the number seven seed Sidney Wood and Budge won in straight sets 6-3, 6-3, 6-3. His final opponent was his friend and doubles partner Gene Mako, who had beaten John Bromwich in the other semi-final. Budge won the first set 6-3 before Mako hit back to win the second 8-6. It was only the fifth set that Budge had lost in the four Grand Slams that year. He would not lose another as he won the final two sets 6-2, 6-1 to become the first person to win a Grand Slam in tennis. Budge was also the youngest man in history to complete the career Grand Slam (the four majors in a career). After the match there were suggestions that Budge had thrown the second set, an accusation that he vehemently denied. "I had too much respect and affection for Gene to treat him as if he were an inferior player who could be given a set for his troubles, rather like a condescending pat on the head." Having won everything he could as an amateur, Budge turned professional, playing his first match at Madison Square Garden on 3 January 1939. He beat Ellsworth Vines 6-3, 6-4, 6-2 in 62 minutes. Allison Danzig writing in the *New York Times* said, "The invincibility associated with the name of Donald Budge as the world's foremost amateur tennis player was affirmed last night with the first appearance in the role of a professional at Madison Square Garden. In the presence of a capacity gathering of 16,725 spectators who paid $47,120 the redheaded giant from Oakland, California ... administered a crushing defeat to Ellsworth Vines, the recognised professional champion." In 1964, Budge was admitted to the Tennis Hall of Fame. In December 1999, Budge was injured in a car crash and never fully recovered. He died on 26 January 2000 at a nursing home in Scranton, Pennsylvania. He was 84.

DID YOU KNOW?

Kenneth Gandar-Dower, Don Budge's opponent in the first round of Wimbledon in 1938, was a Renaissance man. He was educated at Harrow where he played cricket, association football, Eton Fives and rackets. He won a scholarship to Trinity College, Cambridge in 1927 to read history. He won Blues in billiards, tennis and real tennis, Rugby Fives, Eton Fives and rackets as well as being chairman of the Trinity debating society. A talented tennis player, he never got past the third round at Wimbledon in any discipline. He ran constantly during matches, earning himself the nickname of The Undying Retriever. In June 1932, he entered the King's Cup Air Race and made one of the first flights from England to India. In 1934, he led an expedition to Mount Kenya and the Aberdare Range to try to capture a marozi, a spotted lion which remains undiscovered. In 1935 and 1936, he lived in the Congo and Kenya. He returned to England in 1937 with a dozen cheetahs, with the idea of bringing cheetah racing to Britain. The first cheetah race in Britain took place at Romford dog track on 11 December 1937 but the effort was doomed to failure because the cheetahs had no real interest in chasing a hare and in any case could not negotiate tight bends. Gandar-Dower played competitive cricket in the 1930s and won the British Amateur Squash championships in 1938. He worked as a war correspondent during the Second World War but on 12 February 1944 two Japanese submarines torpedoed the ship he was on, the SS *Khedive Ismail* bound for Colombo. It sank with the loss of 1,297 lives including Kenneth Gandar-Dower. He was 35 years old.

ONLY

PLAYER TO WIN GENTLEMEN'S SINGLES,
GENTLEMEN'S DOUBLES AND
MIXED DOUBLES TITLES ON ONLY
VISIT TO WIMBLEDON

**BOBBY RIGGS, GENTLEMEN'S SINGLES, THE CHAMPIONSHIPS, CHURCH ROAD,
WIMBLEDON, SURREY SW, ENGLAND. FRIDAY, 7 JULY 1939; GENTLEMEN'S DOUBLES,
THE CHAMPIONSHIPS, CHURCH ROAD, WIMBLEDON, SURREY SW, ENGLAND.
SATURDAY, 8 JULY 1939; MIXED DOUBLES, THE CHAMPIONSHIPS, CHURCH ROAD,
WIMBLEDON, SURREY SW, ENGLAND. SATURDAY, 8 JULY 1939**

At the last Wimbledon Championships before the outbreak of war, a
brash American called Bobby Riggs arrived in town. In 1939, Riggs
was rated the number one player in the world, a title he would hold as
a professional in 1946 and 1947. Something of a precious player, Riggs
was the first person to win California's State High School Singles trophy
three times. Aged 18, Riggs won the Southern California Men's title
and ended the year ranked fourth among male US tennis players. Rival
Jack Kramer said of him, "Riggs was a great champion. He beat Segura.
He beat Budge when Don was just a little bit past his peak. On a long
tour, as up and down as Vines was, I'm not so sure that Riggs wouldn't
have played Elly very close. I'm sure he would have beaten Gonzales –
Bobby was too quick, he had too much control for Pancho – and Laver
and Rosewall and Hoad. He could keep the ball in play, and he could
find ways to control the bigger, more powerful opponent. He could pin
you back by hitting long, down the lines, and then he'd run you ragged
with chips and drop shots. He was outstanding with a volley from either
side, and he could lob as well as any man … he could also lob on the run.
He could disguise it, and he could hit winning overheads. They weren't
powerful, but they were always on target."

In 1938, Riggs was selected for the American Davis Cup team. The
following year, he arrived at Wimbledon. The reigning champion Don
Budge was unable to compete as he had turned professional at the end of
the 1938 season. In the Gentlemen's Singles, Riggs was seeded number

two. In the first round, he beat Indian qualifier Jagan Dhamija 6-3, 6-0, 6-4. He saw off Briton Ted Avory 6-4, 6-4, 6-2 in the second round. New Zealander Cam Malfroy was Riggs's third opponent and Riggs triumphed 8-6, 11-9, 6-2 to meet Britain's Ronnie Shayes in the fourth round. Shayes went down 7-5, 6-8, 6-4, 6-3. Riggs then came up against Ghaus Mohammad, **the first Indian to reach the quarter-finals at Wimbledon**. He did not prove too much of a hassle for Riggs, who won 6-2, 6-2, 6-2. In the semi-final, Riggs played the number four seed Franjo Punčec from the Kingdom of Yugoslavia. Riggs won 6-2, 6-3, 6-4 to move into the final, where he met fellow American Elwood Cooke, who was seeded number six. Riggs beat Cooke 2-6, 8-6, 3-6, 6-3, 6-2 to win the Gentlemen's Singles title. Riggs and Cooke combined to enter the Gentlemen's Doubles – the defending champions Don Budge and Gene Mako, having turned professional, were ineligible to compete. The German pair of Henner Henkel and Georg von Metaxa (he was actually born in Austria-Hungary) were seeded number one, with Riggs and Cooke number two. In the first round, the Americans played the British pair of Eric Filby and Laurie Shaffi and won 6-3, 6-3, 6-2. Their second-round opponents were the British qualifiers C.F. Hall and F.G. Hill and Riggs and Cooke won 6-2, 6-1, 6-3. More Britons – George Godsell and Pat Sherwood – faced the Americans but lost 6-3, 6-3, 6-3. In the quarter-finals, Riggs and Cooke faced their fourth set of Britons – Henry Billington (the grandfather of Tim Henman) and Patrick Hughes. The Britons took the Americans to five sets but ultimately Riggs and Cooke won 6-3, 3-6, 6-8, 6-2, 11-9. Their semi-final opponents were two of the French Four Musketeers, Jean Borotra and Jacques "Toto" Brugnon. The Americans dropped one set but saw off the French 6-4, 3-6, 6-2, 6-3. More Britons faced the Americans in the final, but Charles Hare and Frank Wild were no match for Riggs and Cooke, who won 6-3, 3-6, 6-3, 9-7. In the Mixed Doubles, Don Budge and Alice Marble were the defending champions so Riggs took Budge's place to play with Marble and they were seeded number two. Riggs's men's doubles partner Elwood Cooke and Sarah Fabyan were the top seeds. Receiving a bye in the first round, Riggs and Marble played the British pair of Cliff Hovell and Denise Huntbach in the second round and won 6-3, 6-1. Another

British pair, Eric Filby and Mary Whitmarsh provided little competition in the third round, losing 6-0, 6-3. In the fourth round, Riggs and Marble beat Bob Mulliken and Sheila Kenyon of Great Britain 6-2, 6-2. In the quarter-final they played more Britons, Jimmy Jones and Ermyntrude Harvey, who took the first set 7-5 but peaked too early and lost the second and third 6-1, 6-3. In the semi-final they again lost the first set – 6-3 – to New Zealander Cam Malfroy and Betty Nuthall but regrouped to win the second and third 6-2, 6-4. In the final Marble and Riggs beat Frank Wilde and Nina Brown 9-7, 6-1.

Oddly, in 1939 Alice Marble also won the Ladies' Singles, Ladies' Doubles and Mixed Doubles although, unlike Riggs, it was not her only visit to Wimbledon. She won the Ladies' Doubles in 1938 and 1939 and Mixed Doubles in 1937, 1938 and 1939. On 17 September 1939, Riggs also won the US National Championships and was runner-up at the French Championships. He won the American title again in 1941 before turning professional. He played his first professional tennis match on 26 December 1941.

DID YOU KNOW?

Neither of the number one seeds in the year that Riggs and Cooke won the Gentlemen's Doubles lived to see the end of the Second World War. Henner Henkel was born on 9 October 1915 in Posen. In 1932 and 1933, he won the German Junior Championships. In 1937, he won the French Championships and with Count Gottfried von Cramm the Men's Doubles. The same year the pair won the Men's Doubles in America, beating the homegrown Don Budge and Gene Mako in straight sets. Henkel played 66 times for Germany in the Davis Cup. Called up, he was killed on 13 January 1943 near Voronezh during the Battle of Stalingrad. He was 27.

Georg von Metaxa was born in Vienna on 7 October 1914, the son of a Greek father and Austrian mother. A wayward boy, he was expelled from several schools before tennis came to his rescue. He reached the final of the 1932 German Boys' Championships, but

---

lost to Henkel. In 1937, von Metaxa won the Austrian National Championships, beating Roderich Menzel in the final. Beginning in 1933, he played 16 matches in the Davis Cup for Austria and, after the Anschluss on 12 March 1938, von Metaxa joined the German Davis Cup team and played 19 matches. He was rated the second-best German player in 1938.

In July 1938, with Henkel, he reached the Wimbledon Gentlemen's Doubles final, which they lost in four sets to the American pair of Don Budge and Gene Mako. When the Second World War began, he was called up into the Wehrmacht. On 12 December 1944, Obergefreiter Georg von Metaxa was killed by American artillery at the town of Arnoldsweiler near Düren, on the Ruhr river in North Rhine-Westphalia, Germany. He was 30.

ONLY
WINNER OF WIMBLEDON GENTLEMEN'S SINGLES CHAMPIONSHIP
SENT TO A CONCENTRATION CAMP

Jean Borotra, Itter Castle, Tyrol, Austria. November 1942

Jean Borotra was one of the Four Musketeers who dominated tennis in the late 1920s and early 1930s. In August 1940, Borotra, a member of *François de la Rocque's Parti Social Français* (PSF), became 1st General Commissioner for Education and Sports in the Vichy government of Marshal Pétain. Borotra was put in charge of the *Révolution nationale*'s efforts in sports policy. In November 1942, Borotra was taken into custody by the Gestapo. He was sent to a concentration camp in Germany before being moved to Itter Castle in North Tyrol until May 1945.

ONLY

WINNER OF WIMBLEDON
GENTLEMEN'S SINGLES CHAMPIONSHIP
AND A PROFESSIONAL GOLF TOURNAMENT

ELLSWORTH VINES, GENTLEMEN'S SINGLES CHAMPIONSHIP, THE
CHAMPIONSHIPS, CHURCH ROAD, WIMBLEDON, SURREY SW, ENGLAND.
SATURDAY, 2 JULY 1932; SOUTHERN CALIFORNIA OPEN CHAMPIONSHIP,
CALIFORNIA, UNITED STATES OF AMERICA. 1945

Born in Los Angeles, California on 28 September 1911 6ft 2½in Henry
Ellsworth Vines, Jr was a talented tennis player. He won the Wimbledon
Men's Singles Championship in 1932, beating Bunny Austin 6-4, 6-2,
6-0, and the US Open Men's Singles Championship on 12 September
1931 and 3 September 1932 at Forest Hills. He reached the Wimbledon
final in 1933 and played his first professional tennis match on 10 January
1934. The match at Madison Square Garden against Bill Tilden was
watched by 14,637 people – then the record for the largest attendance at a
tennis match – and Tilden emerged victorious 8-6, 6-3, 6-2. The contest
between the two men saw Vines win 47 matches and Tilden 26, with the
tour raising $243,000 – then the highest amount for a professional tour.
Vines won his last tournament, the United States Pro Championship at
Beverly Hills Tennis Club, on 22 October 1939 and played his last match
in May 1940 at the age of 28 years, seven months, before turning his
hand to golf, having become bored with tennis. He became a professional
golfer in 1942 and three years later won the Southern California Open
Championship. He died on St Patrick's Day, 1994.

DID YOU KNOW?

The only players to win a Grand Slam are Don Budge (1938),
Maureen Connolly (1953), Rod Laver (1962, 1969), Margaret Court
(1970) and Steffi Graf (1988).

LAST
FRENCHMAN TO WIN WIMBLEDON GENTLEMEN'S SINGLES TITLE

LAST
WIMBLEDON GENTLEMEN'S SINGLES TITLE-WINNER TO WEAR
LONG TROUSERS ON COURT

YVON PETRA, GENTLEMEN'S SINGLES, THE CHAMPIONSHIPS, CHURCH ROAD, WIMBLEDON, SURREY SW, ENGLAND. FRIDAY, 5 JULY 1946

The 6ft 5in Frenchman Yvon Petra (actually born in Cholon, French Indochina, now near Saigon, Vietnam, where his parents were civil servants in the colonial government) was the last of the male tennis stars to wear long trousers when he was playing. In the late 1930s he was regarded as the best player in France. During the Second World War his knee was badly injured during a battle with the Germans and he spent five years in a prisoner of war camp. He never thought that he would get back on the tennis court, but in 1946 he fought his way through to the Wimbledon Gentlemen's Singles final and beat Australian Jeffrey Brown 6-2, 6-4, 7-9, 5-7, 6-2. The stadium had not been completely repaired after being bombed by the Luftwaffe in the Second World War.

ONLY
WIMBLEDON OFFICIAL SACKED FOR DESIGNING A PLAYER'S DRESS

TED TINLING, LONDON, ENGLAND. 1949

Cuthbert Collingwood – known as Teddy – Tinling was born on 23 June 1910 in Eastbourne, Sussex. In 1924, he umpired a match that featured Suzanne Lenglen and he was taken by her sense of style. In 1937, he designed his first tennis dress for her, for her last world tour. He became an in-demand name in haute couture rivalling Hardy Amies and Norman Hartnell. In 1927, he landed a job at Wimbledon which required him to escort players from their dressing rooms to Centre Court and Number One Court for their matches. In 1947, he designed his first Wimbledon tennis dress for Joy Gannon. Two years later, "Gorgeous Gussy" Moran asked Tinling to design her tennis dresses and the underwear to go with them for Wimbledon. The resulting outfit including the lace-trimmed panties caused outrage. Tinling was accused of bringing "vulgarity and sin into tennis" and was sacked from his Wimbledon role. He continued to design dresses for lady players and was reinstated at Wimbledon as the head of the liaison committee in 1982. Tinling died on 23 May 1990 in Cambridge. He was unmarried.

FIRST
BLACK PERSON TO PLAY IN THE
UNITED STATES NATIONAL CHAMPIONSHIPS

Althea Gibson, United States National Championships, West Side Tennis Club, One Tennis Place, Forest Hills, Queens, New York 11375 United States of America. Monday, 28 August 1950

Born in the summer of 1927 at Silver, Clarendon County, South Carolina, Althea Neale Gibson was the daughter of sharecroppers who moved to Harlem in 1930 during the Great Depression. Her father beat her, so she spent time living in a home for abused children. In 1940, her neighbours clubbed together to pay for tennis lessons for her. She was not grateful. She thought it a sport for weeds. "I kept wanting to fight the other player every time I started to lose a match," she said. In spite of her pugilistic nature, in 1941 she won her first competition – the

American Tennis Association (ATA) New York State Championship. In 1947, she won the first of ten consecutive national ATA women's titles. She had no doubts about her talent. "I didn't need to prove that to myself. I only wanted to prove it to my opponents," she said. "I knew that I was an unusual, talented girl, through the grace of God." She was coached by Walter Johnson, who would also go on to mentor Arthur Ashe. In 1949, she became the first black woman to participate in the United States Tennis Association's National Indoor Championships. She reached the last eight. Like Ashe, she won a sporting scholarship to go to university – in her case Florida Agricultural and Mechanical University, an historically black university in Tallahassee. The following year, she was invited to play in the United States National Championships where she made her first appearance on her 23rd birthday. She was eliminated in the second round in a rain-delayed, three-set match against Louise Brough, the reigning Wimbledon champion and former US National winner and number three seed in the tournament. Journalist Lester Rodney said, "No Negro player, man or woman, has ever set foot on one of these courts. In many ways, it is even a tougher personal Jim Crow-busting assignment than was Jackie Robinson's when he first stepped out of the Brooklyn Dodgers dugout."

ONLY

TENNIS PLAYER BANNED FOR LIFE BY USLTA

EARL COCHELL, MEN'S SINGLES, UNITED STATES NATIONAL CHAMPIONSHIPS, WEST SIDE TENNIS CLUB, ONE TENNIS PLACE, FOREST HILLS, QUEENS, NEW YORK 11375, UNITED STATES OF AMERICA. MONDAY, 27 AUGUST 1951

Earl Harry Cochell was born on 18 May 1922 and turned professional in 1940. In 1951, he was playing in the Men's Singles at the United States National Championships when he reached the fourth round, having beaten Briton Tony Mottram in the third, and was drawn against Gardnar Mulloy, the number 11 seed. Cochell won the first set 6-4 but then calls began to go against him and he made his disagreement vocal. The crowd did not see this as behaviour appropriate for the surroundings so began booing him. At one point, he tried to climb into the umpire's chair to grab the microphone to let the crowd know what he thought of them. Prevented from doing this, he began playing badly deliberately – serving underarm and holding his racquet in his left hand. Unsurprisingly, he lost the last three sets 6-2, 6-1, 6-2. The tournament referee S. Ellsworth Davenport went to have a word with Cochell in the changing room afterwards and was met with a mouthful of obscenity. Two days later, the executive committee of the United States Lawn Tennis Association announced Cochell's punishment for his unsportsmanlike behaviour and abuse of the referee – he was banned for life. The ban was lifted in 1962 but by then Cochell was too old to compete.

FIRST

FRED PERRY FASHION LINE
The Championships, Church Road, Wimbledon, Surrey SW, England. 1952

Austrian footballer Theodore "Tibby" Wegner contacted Fred Perry after the Second World War to work with him on a new product – an anti-perspirant worn on the wrist. Perry made a few tweaks and introduced the sweatband. The next project they worked on was a sports shirt manufactured from white knitted cotton pique with short sleeves and a buttoned placket like René Lacoste's. They were introduced at Wimbledon in 1952 and were a runaway success. In the late 1950s coloured versions of the shirt were introduced for table tennis where white shirts are not allowed. The shirts carry a laurel wreath logo, which is based on Wimbledon's original symbol. In the 1960s, Fred Perry shirts became synonymous with mods. The business was so successful that Perry and Wegner sold their interest in it to Charles McIntosh in 1961. The Japanese company Hit Union bought the Perry company in 1995.

FIRST

WOMAN TO ACHIEVE A GRAND SLAM

Maureen Connolly, Women's Singles, Australian Open, Kooyong Lawn Tennis Club, 489 Glenferrie Road, Kooyong, Victoria 3144, Australia. Saturday, 17 January 1953; Women's Singles, French Championships, Stade Roland-Garros, 2 Avenue Gordon Bennett, 75016 Paris, France. Saturday, 30 May 1953; Ladies' Singles, The Championships, Church Road, Wimbledon, Surrey SW, England. Saturday, 4 July 1953; Women's Singles, United States National Championships, West Side Tennis Club, One Tennis Place, Forest Hills, Queens, New York 11375 United States of America. Monday, 7 September 1953

Born in San Diego, California on 17 September 1934, Maureen Catherine Connolly could have been a showjumper or jockey but her mother could not afford riding lessons so Connolly turned to tennis. After switching from her left hand to her right (although she continued to write as a southpaw) on the advice of coach Wilbur Folsom, she was ready to take on the tennis world from 1944. She began to play three hours a day, five days a week. "Any championship career has foundation stones," she said. "Mine were slavish work and driving determination." Allison Danzig of the *New York Times* said, "Maureen, with her perfect timing, fluency, balance and confidence, has developed the most overpowering stroke of its kind the game has known."

Connolly won more than 50 competitions before her 15th birthday, losing just four matches. In August 1951, she became the youngest player on an American Wightman Cup team and on 5 September that year,

Connolly became the youngest winner of the US Women's National Singles Championship at 16 years, 11 months and 19 days when she beat Shirley Fry, 6-3, 1-6, 6-4, at Forest Hills. (She retained that record until 1979 when Tracy Austin won the title at 16 years, 8 months and 28 days. In 1997, Martina Hingis won her first US Open at 16 years, 11 months, 8 days pushing Connolly into third place.) Connolly kept her title in 1952, beating Doris Hart 6-3, 7-5 in the final.

Before her first trip to Wimbledon in 1951, she spent three months working in a newspaper office to earn the money to buy a new wardrobe for the trip. "All I ever see is my opponent," she said. "You could set off dynamite in the next court and I wouldn't notice." Connolly won her first Wimbledon in 1952, despite having a shoulder injury and ignoring the advice of her coach, Eleanor Tennant, to quit. The argument broke the relationship between the two. Connolly beat Louise Brough in the final, 7-5, 6-3. In January 1953, she began her Grand Slam, winning at the Australian Open when seeded number one. On her way to the final she did not drop a set and lost just ten games – four sets were won 6-0. In the final she played the number two seed Julie Sampson and won 6-3, 6-2. In the Ladies' Doubles, Connolly combined with Sampson to beat the Australian pair of Mary Hawton and Beryl Penrose 6-4, 6-2. In the Mixed Doubles Sampson and Rex Hartwig beat Connolly and Ham Richardson 6-4, 6-3.

Four months later, the action moved onto Paris, France. Connolly, seeded number one, beat the number two seed and defending champion Doris Hart in the final 6-2, 6-4. At Wimbledon, Connolly successfully defended her title, again beating Hart in the final, 8-6, 7-5 without dropping a set all tournament. Before the final Connolly had lost only eight games. Hart was Connolly's opponent once again in the match that gave her a Grand Slam – the US National Championships final. It took Connolly just 43 minutes to beat Hart 6-2, 6-4. Again, Connolly achieved her feat without dropping a set all tournament and it was her third straight United States National Championships victory. In 1951, 1952 and 1953, the Associated Press named her Woman Athlete of the Year.

On 3 July 1954, Connolly beat Brough 6-2, 7-5 to win her third Wimbledon in a row. On 20 July 1954, the day after winning her last tournament, the US Clay Court Championships at River Forest, Illinois, Connolly was riding her horse known as Colonel Merryboy when the frightened equine collided with a cement lorry at Mission Valley Polo Grounds near San Diego, California. Connolly suffered a compound fracture to her right fibula and torn muscles in her calf. She said later, "I knew immediately I'd never play again." She was correct. Her tennis career was over at 19. She officially retired from tennis in February 1955. Connolly sued the cement lorry's owners for negligence. On 17 December 1957, the Supreme Court of California unanimously affirmed a $95,000 award of compensation. In 1966, Connolly was diagnosed with ovarian cancer. On 4 June 1969, she underwent a third operation for a stomach tumour at Baylor Hospital in Dallas, Texas and she died in Dallas, on 21 June, aged 34. Connolly was inducted into the International Tennis Hall of Fame in 1969. In her autobiography, *Forehand Drive*, published in 1957, she wrote, "I have always believed greatness on a tennis court was my destiny, a dark destiny, at times, where the court became my secret jungle and I a lonely, fear-stricken hunter. I was a strange little girl armed with hate, fear, and a Golden Racket."

DID YOU KNOW?

San Diego sportswriter Nelson Fisher nicknamed Connolly "Little Mo" when she was 11 after he suggested her stroke play was similar to the firepower of battleship USS *Missouri*, known as "Big Mo".

ONLY

GRAND SLAM WINNER TO WIN AN OLYMPIC ICE HOCKEY MEDAL

ONLY

AFRICAN TO WIN GENTLEMEN'S SINGLES

ONLY

EGYPTIAN CITIZEN TO WIN A
GRAND SLAM TOURNAMENT

ONLY

PLAYER TO WIN GENTLEMEN'S SINGLES
WHILE WEARING GLASSES

Jaroslav Drobný, St Moritz, Switzerland. Sunday, 8 February 1948;
Gentlemen's Singles, The Championships, Church Road, Wimbledon,
Surrey SW, England. Friday, 2 July 1954

Czechoslovakian Jaroslav Drobný was born in Prague on 12 October 1921. Beginning in 1938 and ending in 1949, he played centre in the Czechoslovakian ice hockey league. He played for his country in the 1948 Olympics and won a silver medal after the match against Canada ended goalless but the Canadians took gold because they had a better overall goal difference – 64 to Czechoslovakia's 62. On 11 July 1949, he left Czechoslovakia to play in the Davis Cup and on 27 July, in Gstaad, Switzerland, he defected. "All I had," Drobný would write later, "was a couple of shirts, the proverbial toothbrush and $50." He was eventually offered Egyptian citizenship and he became a British subject in 1959, but before that, in 1954, he became the only player with African citizenship to win the Wimbledon Championships (Roger Federer holds dual South African and Swiss citizenship but represents Switzerland in sports events). In 1946, he reached the Wimbledon semi-final and in 1951 and 1952, he won the French Open. Two years later, he won the Gentlemen's Singles at Wimbledon, beating Ken Rosewall 13-11, 4-6, 6-2, 9-7. Drobný was the first left-hander to win Wimbledon since Norman Brookes. While playing ice hockey he received an eye injury which meant he played tennis wearing tinted prescription glasses – the only man to win a Wimbledon singles' title sporting spectacles. He received the trophy from Marina, Duchess of Kent. He died on 13 September 2001. Drobný was inducted into the International Tennis Hall of Fame in 1983.

DID YOU KNOW?

Jaroslav Drobný was the only player to appear at Wimbledon under four different national identities. In 1938, aged 16, he started for his native Czechoslovakia. Then after the Germans occupied the country he represented the Protectorate of Bohemia and Moravia. After the war, he became Czech again before becoming Egyptian and then British for his last year at The Championships.

FIRST

BLACK PERSON TO WIN A GRAND SLAM TOURNAMENT

ALTHEA GIBSON, FRENCH CHAMPIONSHIPS, STADE ROLAND-GARROS, 2 AVENUE GORDON BENNETT, 75016 PARIS, FRANCE. SATURDAY, 26 MAY 1956

Six years after she became the first black person to play in the United States National Championships (see 1950), Althea Gibson, the number three seed, won the Ladies' Singles crown at the French Championships. In the first round, she bested Frenchwoman Raymonde Gimault 6-1, 6-1. In the next round, her opponent was Věra Suková from Czechoslovakia and Gibson won 6-4, 6-2. In round three she was drawn against another European, Ginette Bucaille, the French number 14 seed, and won easily, 6-1, 6-1. The quarter-final brought another European opponent, Britain's number six seed Shirley Bloomer, who would be the top-ranked singles player in Britain in 1957. Shirley's game did not manage to bloom and Gibson won 6-2, 6-1. In the semi-final, Briton Angela Buxton in her best performance in the competition took Gibson to three sets but lost 2-6, 6-0, 6-4. In the final, Gibson met a Briton for the third consecutive match but reigning champion Angela Mortimer went down 6-0 in the first set before pushing Gibson in the second, losing only 12-10. The match took one hour and 45 minutes to complete. Gibson's win was her first in her fifth meeting with Mortimer. The Associated Press reported: "Miss Gibson was so happy at beating Miss Mortimer for the first time that she leaped over the net to put her arms around her erstwhile jinx."

FIRST

UNSEEDED WINNER OF UNITED STATES NATIONAL CHAMPIONSHIPS MEN'S SINGLES TITLE

Mal Anderson, Men's Singles, United States National Championships, West Side Tennis Club, One Tennis Place, Forest Hills, Queens, New York 11375, United States of America. Sunday, 8 September 1957

Since the introduction of seeding in 1927, no unseeded player had ever won the US Men's Singles title. That record came to an end in 1957 with the right-handed Australian Mal Anderson. Born in 1935, he began playing tennis when he was eight and started taking the game seriously eight years later. In 1956 (and in 1958), he reached the semi-finals at Wimbledon. In 1957, he was not regarded as a hopeful to win the Men's Singles title at the United States National Championships. Anderson did not meet a seeded player until the fourth round, when he defeated the number two seed Richard Savitt in straight sets 6-4, 6-3, 6-1. In the quarter-finals, he beat the Chilean Luis Ayala 6-1, 6-3, 6-1. Anderson was taken to five sets in the semi-final by the number three seed Sven Davidson but beat him 5-7, 6-2, 4-6, 6-3, 6-4. In the final, he met the number one seed and fellow Australian Ashley Cooper. Anderson upped his game even more and took the title, beating Cooper 10-8, 7-5, 6-4. Earlier in the year, he had reached the semi-finals of the Australian Championships and won the French Championship Doubles, with Cooper. In 1958, Anderson was a finalist at the Australian Championships and US Championships, losing on both occasions to Cooper.

FIRST

BLACK WOMAN TO WIN WIMBLEDON LADIES' SINGLES TITLE

FIRST

BLACK WOMAN TO RETAIN
WIMBLEDON LADIES' SINGLES TITLE

Althea Gibson, Ladies' Singles, The Championships,
Church Road, Wimbledon, Surrey SW, England.
Saturday, 6 July 1957; Ladies' Singles, The
Championships, Church Road, Wimbledon, Surrey
SW, England. Saturday, 5 July 1958

In 1956, 5ft 11in Althea Gibson was seeded number four at Wimbledon
and made the quarter-finals, where she lost to Shirley Fry, the eventual
winner. A year later, Fry did not return to defend her title and Gibson
was seeded number one. She received a bye in the first round and met
Hungarian Zsuzsa Körmöczy in the second round. Gibson won 6-4, 6-4.
In the next round, she met Australian Margaret Hellyer and won 6-4,
6-2. In the fourth round, she beat Hong Kong-born Gem Hoahing 6-1,
6-1, then, in the quarter-final she beat South African Sandra Reynolds
6-3, 6-4. Gibson's semi-final opponent was Briton Christine Truman
but she was no match for the American, who won 6-1, 6-1. Her final
opponent was fellow American Darlene Hard, the number five seed.
Gibson won relatively easily in straight sets – 6-3, 6-2. Gibson was
the first black winner and the first to receive a trophy from the Queen.
"Shaking hands with the Queen of England," she said, "was a long way
from being forced to sit in the coloured section of the bus."

The following year, Gibson was again seeded number one. She
began her defence of her crown against Hellyer, who she had beaten the
previous year on the way to victory. This time – the second round – she
won with relative ease 6-0, 6-2. In the third round, she took an age to
overcome Mexican Yola Ramírez, finally winning 9-7 in the first set
before a comparatively easy 6-2 win in the second. In the fourth round
she played Australian Lorraine Coghlan and Gibson sailed through 6-0,
6-2. The quarter-final was against Shirley Bloomer, the number five
seeded Briton she had beaten in the same round two years earlier in her

French Championships campaign. On this occasion, Bloomer put up more of a fight taking the match to three sets. Gibson eventually won 6-3, 6-8, 6-2 to line up a semi-final against another Briton, Ann Haydon. It was an easy 6-2, 6-0 victory for the American. Her final opponent – like the quarter-final – was the same woman she had beaten to take the French title, Angela Mortimer who was unseeded. Gibson won 8-6, 6-2, but she was unable to defend her title in 1959 because she had turned professional.

FIRST

BLACK WOMAN TO WIN
UNITED STATES NATIONAL CHAMPIONSHIPS
WOMEN'S SINGLES TITLE IN CONSECUTIVE YEARS

Althea Gibson, Women's Singles, United States National Championships, West Side Tennis Club, One Tennis Place, Forest Hills, Queens, New York 11375 United States of America. Sunday, 8 September 1957; Women's Singles, United States National Championships, West Side Tennis Club, One Tennis Place, Forest Hills, Queens, New York 11375 United States of America. Sunday, 7 September 1958

In 1956, Althea Gibson was seeded number two and finished runner-up to Shirley Fry in the United States National Championships Ladies' Singles tournament. The next year, she was seeded number one and determined to show the faith bestowed upon her by the seeders was justified. In the quarter-finals she played Australian Mary Hawton, the number eight seed, and won 6-2, 6-2. Her semi-final opponent was third seed Dorothy Knode and Gibson triumphed by the same winning margin. Her opponent in the final was American Louise Brough, the number two seed. Gibson won 6-3, 6-2. A year later, Gibson returned to defend her title. In the quarter-final, she played Briton Christine Truman, the number seven seed. The first set was a mammoth 20-gamer with Gibson finally winning 11-9 before a more comfortable 6-1 win the second set. In the semi-final, she came across fellow American Beverly

Baker Fleitz and won 6-4, 6-2. In the final she played American Darlene Hard, her 1957 Wimbledon opponent. Hard won the first set 6-3 but Gibson upped her game to take the second and third sets – 6-1, 6-2 – and the title. Vice President Richard M. Nixon presented Gibson with her trophy. The feat of a black woman winning back-to-back US Open titles would not be repeated until Venus Williams in 2000 and 2001.

FIRST

AUSTRALIAN TO WIN A GRAND SLAM TOURNAMENT OVERSEAS

Margaret Smith, Women's Singles, French Championships, Roland-Garros, 2 Avenue Gordon Bennett, 75016 Paris, France. Saturday, 2 June 1962; Women's Singles, US National Championships, West Side Tennis Club, 1 Tennis Place, Forest Hills, NY 11375 United States of America. Monday, 10 September 1962

Born on 16 July 1942 at Albury, New South Wales, Margaret Smith began playing tennis when she was eight. She won her first Australian Championship in 1960 when she was 18 and repeated the feat in 1961, 1962, 1963, 1964, 1965, 1966, 1969, 1970, 1971 and 1973. In 1962, she became the first Australian to win a Grand Slam tournament abroad when she won the Women's Singles at the French Open. She was seeded second and in the second round she beat Austrian Maria Lehrer. In the next round, she soundly beat South African Jean Forbes 6-0, 6-2. In the fourth round, another Australian, Mary Renetta Hawton, fell 6-1, 6-3 to Smith. In the quarter-final West German Edda Buding, the seventh seed, proved more of a challenge as Smith won 6-2, 6-4. In the semi-final she was drawn against South African Renee Schuurman, who was seeded sixth. Smith won a tight battle 8-6, 6-3. In the final she played fellow Australian Lesley Turner, the number 13 seed, who had beaten number one seed Briton Ann Haydon (later Jones) in three sets in her semi-final. Smith won the first set 6-3 before Turner took the second set by the same margin. The third and final set was won by Smith, 7-5. Three months later, she took her second major of the year when she won the US Open. Seeded number one, in the quarter-final, she beat South African Sandra Reynolds Price, the number eight seed, 6-3, 6-3 to set up a semi-final with the third seed Argentinian Maria Bueno. Smith lost the first set 8-6 before recovering to take the next two sets 6-3, 6-4. In the final, Smith met American Darlene Hard who had won the title in 1960 and 1961 but was seeded fifth. It was a tough match but Smith came out on top 9-7, 6-4. Hard hit 16 double faults in the final.

FIRST
FEDERATION CUP
FEDERATION CUP, QUEEN'S CLUB, PALLISER ROAD, HAMMERSMITH, LONDON W14 9EQ, ENGLAND. MONDAY, 17 - THURSDAY, 20 JUNE 1963

The female version of the Davis Cup was first contested by 16 countries in London in the summer of 1963 a week before Wimbledon. It was created to celebrate the 50th anniversary of the International Tennis Federation and was won in the first year by the United States. There was no prize money that year and contestants had to pay for themselves. In 1995, it changed its name to the Fed Cup. Australia, the Czech Republic and the United States are **the only countries to have held both Davis Cup and Fed Cup in the same year**.

FIRST
WIMBLEDON TOURNAMENT IN WHICH
PLAYERS HAD TO WEAR WHITE
THE CHAMPIONSHIPS, CHURCH ROAD, WIMBLEDON, SURREY SW, ENGLAND. MONDAY, 24 JUNE 1963 – MONDAY, 8 JULY 1963

The 1963 Wimbledon Championships were the 77th time the competition had been held. The winter of 1962–1963 had been the coldest on record apart from 1683–1684 and 1739–1740. Football was badly affected, with some matches being rescheduled up to ten times. The Pools Panel was established to adjudicate – or guess – on games for the football pools. The season was delayed by four weeks and some matches were played only the day before the rescheduled FA Cup Final. Ninety-four National Hunt horse meets were cancelled. By the time Wimbledon came around, the weather was still poor and the tournament was completed in cold and wet weather conditions. Play on the final Saturday was cancelled due to the rain and the Ladies' Singles, the Gentlemen's and Ladies' Doubles and the Mixed Doubles finals were not finished until Monday, 8 July.

DID YOU KNOW?

American Andre Agassi refused to play at Wimbledon from 1988 until 1990 because he did not like the dress code and what he regarded as a "stuffy" atmosphere.

FIRST

AUSTRALIAN TO WIN WIMBLEDON LADIES' SINGLES

MARGARET SMITH, LADIES' SINGLES, THE CHAMPIONSHIPS, CHURCH ROAD, WIMBLEDON, SURREY SW, ENGLAND. MONDAY, 8 JULY 1963

Having won two majors the year before, Margaret Smith was the number one seed at Wimbledon. Given a bye in the first round, she easily beat Canadian Louise Brown 6-1, 6-1 in the second. In the next round, she was drawn against Swede Katarina Bartholdson and had another simple victory 6-1, 6-0. In the fourth round, Argentinian Norma Baylon pressed her but Smith won 6-3, 6-3. Eighth seed, South African Renee Schuurman was her quarter-final opponent and she took the first set 6-3 before Smith regained her form and won 6-0, 6-1. In the semi-final, she met number four seed Darlene Hard and won 6-3, 6-3. In the final, she came up against the unseeded Billie Jean Moffitt who had beaten Ann Jones 6-4, 6-4 in the semi-final (who had herself overcome the young Virginia Wade 6-3, 9-7 in the second round). Smith won 6-3, 6-4 to complete the career Grand Slam in singles – adding Wimbledon to the Australian, French and US titles.

FIRST

BLACK MAN TO PLAY IN THE
DAVIS CUP FOR THE UNITED STATES

Arthur Ashe, Davis Cup, United States v Venezuela, Cherry Hills Country Club, 4125 South University Boulevard, Cherry Hills Village, Colorado 80113 United States of America. Sunday, 15 September 1963

Arthur Ashe made his Davis Cup debut on the third day of the series against Venezuela, which the United States won by five games to love. Ashe played Orlando Bracamonte and won 6-1, 6-1, 6-0. On 6 March 1981, Ashe made his debut as captain of the US Davis Cup team, playing Mexico. He played his last Davis Cup match on 8 October 1978 at Gothenburg, Sweden and beat Kjell Johansson 6-2, 6-0, 7-5.

ONLY

GRAND SLAM WINNER AND
WOMEN'S PROFESSIONAL GOLF TOUR PLAYER

Althea Gibson, Women's Singles, French Championships, Stade Roland-Garros, 2 Avenue Gordon Bennett, 75016 Paris, France. Saturday, 26 May 1956; Ladies Professional Golf Association, United States of America. 1964

In 1958, after winning 56 national and international singles and doubles titles, Althea Gibson retired from amateur tennis. In 1964, she became the first black woman to join the Ladies Professional Golf Association

(LPGA) tour. Racism was still rife in America and many clubs refused to let her play and several of those that did insisted she get changed in the car park. In spite of this appalling treatment, for five years she was one of the LPGA's top earners. Her highest ranking was 27th in 1966. She retired from professional golf at the end of the 1978 season. When the Open Era in tennis started, she started entering major tournaments but age was against her. A similar problem faced her in the golf world. In 1987, aged 60, she came out of retirement with a desire to become the oldest player on the professional tour, but was not good enough any more to be accepted. During her tennis career Gibson won 11 Grand Slam tournaments – five singles titles, five doubles titles, and one mixed doubles title. Many paid tribute to her. Billie Jean King commented, "Her road to success was a challenging one but I never saw her back down." The only black mayor of New York City, David Dinkins, said, "To anyone, she was an inspiration, because of what she was able to do at a time when it was enormously difficult to play tennis at all if you were black." Venus Williams added, "I am honoured to have followed in such great footsteps. Her accomplishments set the stage for my success, and through players like myself and Serena and many others to come, her legacy will live on." Althea Gibson died of a urinary tract infection at East Orange General Hospital, East Orange, New Jersey, United States on 28 September 2003. She was 76.

———◆◈◆———

ONLY

PLAYER TO APPEAR AT LADIES' SINGLES

TOURNAMENT WITH HER PHONE NUMBER
ON HER KNICKERS

PAT STEWART, LADIES' SINGLES, THE CHAMPIONSHIPS, CHURCH ROAD, WIMBLEDON, LONDON SW19 5AE, ENGLAND. 1964

In a supposed attempt to boost her social life, American Pat Stewart appeared with her telephone number embroidered on her underwear. In the second round, she beat Frenchwoman Sue Chatrier 3-6, 6-0, 6-3 but in the third round she lost to Margaret Court 6-3, 6-0.

FIRST

PLAYER TO WIN A TOURNAMENT
WITH A METAL RACQUET

BILLIE JEAN KING, LADIES' SINGLES, THE CHAMPIONSHIPS, CHURCH ROAD, WIMBLEDON, LONDON SW19 5AE, ENGLAND. SATURDAY, 8 JULY 1967

Billie Jean King won the 1967 Wimbledon Ladies' title using a Wilson T-2000 aluminium model racquet. King retained her title, beating Ann Jones 6-3, 6-4. That year she also won the US Championships using the same racquet. Wilson did not generously compensate King for testing their equipment. When the Open Era arrived, they upped her money from $500 to $1,500. King asked for an autographed racquet to be produced but Wilson refused because they already had one promoted by Maureen Connolly and did not believe that there was room for two women's tennis racquets on the market.

LAST

AMATEUR US NATIONAL CHAMPIONSHIPS

US National Championships, West Side Tennis Club, One Tennis Place, Forest Hills, Queens, New York 11375 United States of America. Wednesday, 30 August – Sunday, 10 September 1967

The 1967 US National Championships was the 87th time the competition had been held, but the winds of change were blowing in tennis and this was the last of the gentlemen players. From 1968, the competition would change its name to the US Open and welcome all-comers. John Newcombe and Billie Jean King took the honours in the Singles' competitions in 1967 and the three Doubles tournaments took place at the Longwood Cricket Club in Brookline, Massachusetts, from 21 to 29 August 1967.

FIRST

OPEN TOURNAMENT

BRITISH HARD COURT CHAMPIONSHIPS, WEST HANTS LAWN TENNIS
CLUB, ROSLIN ROAD SOUTH, BOURNEMOUTH, DORSET BH3 7EF ENGLAND.
MONDAY, 22 APRIL 1968

After the 1967 demonstration tournament for professionals at Wimbledon, the Open Era began at the seaside. **The first point in the Open Era** was won by Briton John Clifford against Australian professional Owen Davidson, but it was the player from Down Under who won the first Open match, 6-2, 6-3, 4-6, 8-6. Oh, and it was raining. On 28 April, Ken Rosewall won the first tournament, beating fellow professional Rod Laver 3-6, 6-2, 6-0, 6-3. Rosewall took home a prize of £1,000 (£18,000 at 2020 values). **The first Open Women's Singles** was won by Virginia Wade who won £300 (£5,500, 2020). Roy Emerson and Rod Laver won **the first Men's Doubles** and received £250 (£4,765, 2020) each. Christine Janes and Nell Truman won **the first Women's Doubles** and received £50 (£900, 2020) for their troubles. Virginia Wade and Bob Howe won the first Mixed Doubles and walked off with £40 (£725, 2020). The first Grand Slam, the newly named French Open, was also won by Rosewall, beating Laver.

FIRST

US OPEN

FIRST

TELEVISED US OPEN

ONLY

BLACK MAN TO WIN US OPEN

US OPEN, WEST SIDE TENNIS CLUB, ONE
TENNIS PLACE, FOREST HILLS, QUEENS, NEW

YORK 11375, UNITED STATES OF AMERICA. THURSDAY, 29 AUGUST 1968 – SUNDAY, 8 SEPTEMBER 1968

The US Open until 1968 had been known as the United States Lawn Tennis Association National Championship and took place at the West Side Tennis Club, which had been founded by 13 players on Central Park West and 88th Street on 22 April 1892. It had three clay courts and a little clubhouse. The courts opened on 11 June 1892. Club membership was $10 initiation cost, $10 annual fee, and the ability to play tennis to a good standard. By the end of the first season the club had 43 members and five courts. The clubhouse consisted of a shed with two dressing rooms and cold showers. Ten years later, the club moved to 117th Street and Amsterdam Avenue near Columbia University where it had space for eight courts. By then, the membership had grown to 110 players. In 1908, it relocated to 238th Street and Broadway where it had room for a dozen grass courts and 15 clay ones. In 1911, the West Side Tennis Club played host to the International Lawn Tennis Challenge (now the Davis Cup), watched by crowds of 3,000 daily. The following year, realising its facilities were inadequate for the crowds, the club moved for the final time to its present site in Forest Hills. In 1915, the United States National Lawn Tennis Association (USNLTA, now USTA) Men's National Championship (later the US Open) moved to the West Side Tennis Club from the Newport Casino. Construction of a 14,000-seat horseshoe-shaped ground began in April 1923 and was opened that August – **America's first tennis stadium**.

The 1968 Open – the 88th staging of the championship – was the first to be shown on television. It was broadcast on CBS with commentary by Bud Collins and former player Dan Kramer, who also commentated at Wimbledon from 1960 until 1973. It was also the first tournament of the Open Era of tennis and there was $100,000 of prize money on offer. The prize for the men was $14,000 while the winner of the Women's Singles would take home $6,000. Arthur Ashe and Virginia Wade won the singles titles. Ashe is the only black man to win the title.

FIRST

LEFT-HANDED PLAYER TO WIN
WIMBLEDON LADIES' SINGLES

LAST

GRAND SLAM SINGLES TOURNAMENT
FOR ANN JONES

**ANN JONES, LADIES' SINGLES, THE CHAMPIONSHIPS, CHURCH ROAD,
WIMBLEDON, LONDON SW19 5AE ENGLAND. FRIDAY, 4 JULY 1969**

Ann Jones lost the finals of Wimbledon and the US Championships in 1967 to Billie Jean King, but in 1969 she got her revenge. Jones was seeded number four while King was number two. In the first round Jones easily saw off Carmen Mandarino of Spain 6-0, 6-1 and bypassed Briton Sue Tutt in the second round by the same margin. Jones's third round opponent was Rosie Darmon from France, who provided little challenge as Jones won 6-1, 6-2. She finally received a stiffer test in the fourth round when Peggy Michel, after losing the first set 6-0, came back to force Jones to a 9-7 second set. In the quarter-final Jones beat the number five seed Nancy Richey 6-2, 7-5. In the semi-final, Jones met the number one seed Australian Margaret Court, who took the first set in a massive 12-10 contest. Jones fought back to take the second and third sets 6-3, 6-2 to set up another contest with Billie Jean King, who was hoping to win the title for the fourth successive year. Jones won the battle though, 6-3, 3-6, 2-6 becoming the first left-handed female player to do so. She received her plate from HRH Princess Anne.

Jones also won the Mixed Doubles title with Australian Fred Stolle and that December was voted the BBC Sports Personality of the Year. She was seeded number one for the 1969 US Open but withdrew before the tournament began and never played another Grand Slam singles tournament.

DID YOU KNOW?

The Beatles halted the dubbing session for their song "Golden Slumbers" to listen to Ann Jones beat Billie Jean King for the Wimbledon title, live on the wireless.

ONLY

PLAYER TO WIN GRAND SLAM TWICE

Rod Laver, v Roy Emerson, Men's Singles, Australian Championships, White City Stadium, Rushcutters Bay, Sydney, New South Wales 2021, Australia. Monday, 15 January 1962; v Roy Emerson, Men's Singles, French Championships, Stade Roland-Garros, 2 Avenue Gordon Bennett, 75016 Paris, France. Saturday, 2 June 1962; v Marty Mulligan, Gentlemen's Singles, The Championships, Church Road, Wimbledon, Surrey SW, England. Friday, 6 July 1962; v Roy Emerson, Men's Singles, United States Lawn Tennis Association National Championships, West Side Tennis Club, One Tennis Place, Forest Hills, Queens, New York 11375, United States of America. Monday, 10 September 1962; Men's Singles, v Andrés Gimeno, Australian Open, Milton Courts, Milton Road, Brisbane, Queensland 4064, Australia. Monday, 27 January 1969; v Ken Rosewall, Men's Singles, French Open, Stade Roland-Garros, 2 Avenue Gordon Bennett, 75016 Paris, France. Sunday, 8 June 1969; v John Newcombe, Gentlemen's Singles, The Championships, Church Road, Wimbledon, London SW19 5AE England. Saturday, 5 July 1969; Open v Tony Roche, Men's Singles, US West Side Tennis Club, One Tennis Place, Forest Hills, Queens, New York 11375, United States of America. Monday, 8 September 1969

Rod Laver was born in rural Rockhampton, Queensland, Australia, on 9 August 1938, the third of four children (two older brothers, one younger sister) of a rancher. His parents, Roy and Melba, met at a tennis tournament in the Queensland town of Dingo. His interest in tennis developed early and a racquet was customised for his small hands, and 5ft 8in Laver went on to win a record 200 tournaments. Laver went to a tennis school run by Harry Hopman, where he got the nickname "Rocket". He later explained, "Going to the clinics made me very nervous at first. Everyone in Australia – and, I thought the world – knew and admired Harry Hopman. He'd been a fine player, then captained the Australian Davis Cup team of Frank Sedgman and Ken McGregor that broke America's post-war grip on the cup in 1950. He was working with Lew Hoad and Ken Rosewall, who were about to burst forth as young world-beaters, and here I was, getting instruction from this important man who was respected everywhere – Wimbledon, Forest Hills, Paris, Rome." The thin Laver added, "I looked like I was on hunger strike most of my life. I was short, skinny and not too quick either. After a couple of days, Hop remarked, 'You're the Rockhampton Rocket, aren't you?' Rocket stuck." Hopman explained, "He was the Rocket – because he wasn't. You know how those nicknames are. Rocket was one of the slowest kids in the class. But his speed picked up as he grew stronger."

In 1953, Laver quit school to focus full time on tennis and three years later won the 1956 US Junior Championship. He spent 1957 serving in the Australian Army. Laver won 54 amateur titles between 1956 and 1962. He began to practise regularly and developed the muscles in his left arm. Measured in 1968, Laver's left wrist was seven inches around, an inch more than his right, and his left forearm was a foot around, an inch and a half more than his right. It was also the same size as that of heavyweight boxing champion Rocky Marciano and an inch and a half larger than that of boxer Floyd Patterson. To strengthen his forehand and fingers, Laver would regularly squeeze a tennis or squash ball.

In 1959, he was chosen for Australia's Davis Cup side and was runner-up at the Gentlemen's Singles at Wimbledon. The following year, he won the Australian Championships beating fellow Australian Neale Fraser in five sets, 5-7, 3-6, 6-3, 8-6, 8-6. In 1961, Laver took just 55 minutes to beat Chuck McKinley to win his first Wimbledon title, 6-3, 6-1, 6-4. He won three Australian titles (1960, 1962, 1969), two French (1962, 1969), four Wimbledon (1961, 1962, 1968, 1969), and two US National/Open (1962, 1969) titles. Four doubles titles were won at the Australian (1959, 1960, 1961, 1969), and one each at the French (1961) and Wimbledon (1971). Mixed doubles titles were won at the French (1961) and Wimbledon (1959, 1960). Red headed, left-handed Laver was **the first player to win $1 million on tour**.

To achieve his first Grand Slam in 1962, he beat fellow Aussie Roy Emerson at three of the four tournaments – at the Australian (8-6, 0-6, 6-4, 6-4), the French (3-6, 2-6, 6-3, 9-7, 6-2) and the US Nationals (6-2, 6-4, 5-7, 6-4). To win Wimbledon, he beat Aussie Marty Mulligan in straight sets (6-2, 6-2, 6-1) in 51 minutes and 35 seconds. "It was a thrill to come off the court knowing I had won all four majors in one year," Laver said. "But I never felt like I was the best, never felt that way. I just happened to have a good year." A report in *The Manchester Guardian* on 7 July 1962 said, "Mulligan would have certainly found [Laver] easier to play last year. The difference between Laver then and Laver now is that he has acquired a far greater discipline, both of stroke and concentration … As well as being the most exciting player at Wimbledon this year, he has also been the most accurate." In December 1961, he was part of the Australian Davis Cup team that easily beat the Italians without the loss of a set – the first time a team had achieved that milestone since 1909.

In 1962, Laver was seeded number one on the outdoor clay courts at Roland-Garros and met Italian Michele Pirro in the second round winning 6-4, 6-0, 6-2. In the third round he beat Englishman Tony Pickard 6-2, 9-7, 4-6, 6-1. Another Italian, Sergio Jacobini, provided the opposition in the fourth round and Laver won 4-6, 6-3, 7-5, 6-1. In the quarter-final Laver faced fellow Australian Marty Mulligan and the match went to five sets with Laver beating his countryman 6-4, 3-6, 2-6, 10-8, 6-2. In the semi-final, Laver came up against the number five seed and another Australian, Neale Fraser, and again Laver was taken to five sets. The end result was 3-6, 6-3, 6-2, 3-6, 7-5 to send Laver through to his second major final of the year and second against Roy Emerson, the number two seed. Again, Laver was taken to five sets but won 3-6, 2-6, 6-3, 9-7, 6-2. Fred Tupper of the *New York Times* opined after Wimbledon, "Laver's one-sided triumph confirmed what everybody has known all along: that the 23-year-old Australian is the best player in amateur tennis today and one of the great ones of our time." After completing a Grand Slam in late December 1962, Laver turned professional, reportedly for $110,000. "I won Wimbledon in 1961 and 1962 and got a £15 voucher and a firm handshake," Laver said. "I just wanted the chance to play against the best players in the world, and that's why I turned pro, plus the financial enumerations were an important part of tennis back in those days."

On 5 January 1963, Laver lost his first professional match to Lew Hoad 6-8, 6-4, 6-3, 8-6. By the middle of the month, Laver had lost his first four professional ties. Rex Lardner wrote in *Sports Illustrated* on 17 September 1962, "Laver uses his wrists more than any other play in history apart from Frank Kovacs and he is the first person to combine a whipping wrist action with near-perfect control. Laver can hit a ball flat, with topspin or underspin, equally well from both sides … Few players have this repertory of strokes, and no player has been able to mask his shots better … But perhaps his greatest ability is to make forcing shots of returns that most players would be happy to get back at all."

Beginning in 1964, Laver triumphed in the US Pro five times in six years. In 1967, he won the Wembley Pro, the French Pro, and US Pro titles, regarded as the professional Grand Slam. He won 69 competitions as a pro, 19 in 1967 alone. With the advent of the Open Era in 1968, Laver found himself playing against the best players in the world again. And he rose magnificently to the challenge. On 5 July 1968, he won **the first Open Gentlemen's Singles at Wimbledon** beating Tony Roche 6-3, 6-4, 6-2. In the 1968 US Open, he was seeded number one but was knocked out in the fourth round in five sets by South African Cliff Drysdale; 1969 came around and the Australian Open was the first Grand Slam of the year. The tournament was played in Brisbane (for the seventh and last time) on Milton's grass courts with 48 men participating. It was the semi-final between Rod Laver and Tony Roche that had everyone talking. Played in 105-degree heat, the match lasted more than four hours. Both players employed an old Australian trick of placing wet cabbage leaves in their hats to help them keep cool. Eventually Laver won 7-5, 22-20, 9-11, 1-6, 6-3. A controversial line call helped Laver take the final set. In the final, he beat Spaniard Andrés Gimeno 6-3, 6-4, 7-5.

At the French Open, the top four seeds were all Australian – Laver, Tony Roche, Ken Rosewall and John Newcombe. The last was the only one who did not reach the semi-finals, being knocked out in the quarter-final by Dutchman Tom Okker in five sets. Laver beat Okker in the semi-final to set up a final opposite Ken Rosewall but his fellow countryman did not present Laver with too many problems as Laver completed half of his second Grand Slam 6-4, 6-3, 6-4 in what Laver called the "best clay court match of my life". He added, "Ken has consistently been my toughest opponent, on any surface, and we've played each other, I don't know, well over 200 times."

The circus moved onto London and the 1969 Wimbledon Championships. The winner of the Gentleman's Singles won £3,000 (£51,200 at 2020 values). Unlike at Roland-Garros, four of the top six seeds were Australian – Laver, Tony Roche, Tom Okker (Holland), Ken Rosewall, Arthur Ashe (United States) and John Newcombe. Laver overcame strong challenges from Stan Smith, Premjit Lall (both of whom took him to five sets), Cliff Drysdale and Arthur Ashe before playing his countryman Newcombe in the final before 15,000 people on a sun-drenched Centre Court. In two hours and 16 minutes, Laver won 6-4, 5-7, 6-4, 6-4 in the first final to go to four sets since 1964. Laver said that this was the toughest of his four Wimbledon finals. "He had that extra shot at just the right time and it swung the pendulum in his favour," Newcombe said. "It didn't surprise me, because he had what it took to win."

The 1969 US Open was beset with rain and it was the last tournament where sets were decided by a two-game advantage. Tie-breaks were introduced in 1970. On wet and slippery grass courts, Laver saw off Dennis Ralston, Roy Emerson and Arthur Ashe. The final was delayed for 95 minutes to allow the court to dry out and officials even hired a helicopter to hover above the stadium to help with the drying. Laver came up against Tony Roche, who managed to settle down quicker in the wet conditions and take the first set 9-7. Roche realised that Laver may be down but he was most certainly not out. "In any final, if you win the first set you feel like you're well on the way, but of all the players, Rod had the unbelievable ability to get out of tough situations and he had such great belief in his game," he said. When they came to change ends, Laver put on a pair of spikes which gave him a better grip. It also led him to win the match 7-9, 6-1, 6-2, 6-2 for his second Grand Slam. After he hit the winning shot, he vaulted the net, something he did not usually do.

In a 23-year career that spanned the amateur, pro, and Open eras, Laver was ranked 11 times in the World Top 10 between 1959 and

1975, reaching number one four times (1961, 1962, 1968 and 1969). In January 2000, the Centre Court Stadium at Melbourne Park, the venue of the Australian Open since 1988, was renamed the Rod Laver Arena. He was inducted into the Sport Australia Hall of Fame in 1985. "Rocket was a guy that had the respect of everybody," said John Newcombe. "The champions of today recognize that he was great, one of the greatest, but they can also sense his strength of humility that there is about him." Laver said, "Tennis-wise, winning this Grand Slam was a lot tougher because of all the good players. Pressure-wise I don't think it was any tougher. There's always pressure when you are playing for something over nine months."

DID YOU KNOW?

Roy Emerson is **the only male player to have completed a career Grand Slam (winning titles at all four Grand Slam events) in both singles and doubles**. His 28 major titles are the all-time record for a male player. Emerson was the first man to win each of the four major titles at least twice in his career. He is one of only eight men to have won all four majors in his career. The others are Fred Perry, Don Budge, Rod Laver, Andre Agassi, Roger Federer, Rafael Nadal and Novak Djokovic. Emerson was the first male player to win a dozen majors. He held that record for 30 years until it was surpassed by Pete Sampras in 2000. Emerson also held the record of six Australian Open Men's Singles titles until 2019 when Novak Djokovic won his seventh title. Emerson won five of them consecutively (1963, 1964, 1965, 1966, 1967). Emerson is one of only five tennis players to have won multiple numbers of Grand Slam tournaments in two tennis disciplines, only matched by Frank Sedgman, Margaret Court, Martina Navratilova and Serena Williams.

FIRST

TIE-BREAK IN GRAND SLAM TENNIS

US OPEN, WEST SIDE TENNIS CLUB, ONE TENNIS PLACE, FOREST HILLS, QUEENS, NEW YORK 11375 UNITED STATES OF AMERICA. WEDNESDAY, 2 – SUNDAY, 13 SEPTEMBER 1970

At the 1970 US Open the tie-break was first used. It used the nine-point shootout (sudden death at 4-4). The USLTA adopted the slogan "We cordially invite you to sudden death in the afternoon at Forest Hills." The system was used until 1974 when the US Open adopted the International Tennis Federation's best-of-12 points system.

FIRST
FEMALE ATHLETE
TO EARN MORE THAN
$100,000 IN A YEAR
BILLIE JEAN KING. 1971

In 1971, Billie Jean King became the first female athlete (in any sport) to earn more than $100,000 in a year. During that year, she won the US Open without losing a set and beating Rose Casals in the final, and also won the Ladies' Doubles and Mixed Doubles at Wimbledon. King played in 31 singles tournaments, winning 112 matches and losing 13.

FIRST
MODERN "BATTLE
OF THE SEXES"
BOBBY RIGGS V MARGARET COURT, SAN DIEGO COUNTRY ESTATES, RAMONA, CALIFORNIA 92065, UNITED STATES OF AMERICA. SUNDAY, 13 MAY 1973

Born in 1918, Bobby Riggs was a skilful tennis player who became the
World No 1 (or co-No 1) three times – as an amateur in 1939, then as
a professional in 1946 and 1947. He was part of the American Davis
Cup-winning team in 1938. In 1939, he was a finalist in the French
Championships and won Wimbledon Gentlemen's Singles and Doubles
(with Elwood Cooke) and the Mixed Doubles with Alice Marble. He
played his first professional tennis match on Boxing Day 1941. After he
retired, Riggs became a notorious self-publicist. He organised several
exhibition matches against past and current champions. In 1973, he
claimed that women players were not as good as their male counterparts
and even at 55 he could beat any of the top females. He challenged Billie
Jean King but she refused to play ball. He turned next to Margaret Court
and she accepted. Court was then 30 and had been rated women's No
1 in 1962, 1963, 1964 (joint with Maria Bueno), 1965, 1969, 1970 and
1973.

The match was arranged for Mother's Day and 5,000 fans turned out
to watch. Not everyone was happy that the match was even going ahead.
"Why should we have to justify ourselves against an old, obnoxious
has-been like Riggs who can't hear, can't see, walks like a duck and is
an idiot besides?" asked Rosie Casals. Riggs took it reasonably seriously.
He jogged, cut down on starch, cigars and alcohol and took 415 vitamin
pills every day in what he called a "rejuvenation process". He said, "This
match is unbelievable. The eyes and ears of the world are on me. I am
the greatest money player in history. I am the finest defensive player
in the game. Margaret is the biggest hitter of the girls. What a match!
Nobody has a clue how it will go. The mystery of the age. What a deal!"
On the morning of the match, Court's young son threw her only pair
of tennis shoes into the lavatory. Designer Teddy Tinling had created a
pastel dress trimmed in the Australian national colours of green and gold
with Court's Christian name embroidered on each side of her collar. The
game was televised by CBS. Riggs presented Court with flowers as he
entered the court and she curtsied in return. Watching the match were
many celebrities including John Wayne, Bill Cosby and O.J. Simpson and
the match was umpired by Ben Press. Court lost 6-2, 6-1 in 57 minutes,

unable to cope with the drop shots and lobs performed by Riggs. She connected on only 18 of 37 first serves and made ten return errors against serve. She later told Jon Henderson of *The Observer*, "I wasn't ready for the showbiz side of it, which I would have been if I'd played team tennis by then. I was used to playing at places like Wimbledon where you could hear a pin drop."

Speaking of the women's professional tour, Riggs said, "What kind of tour is it if the best player can't beat a guy with one foot in the grave?" Neil Amdur (Chris Evert's ghostwriter) of the *New York Times* said, "The victory was the latest and perhaps most amazing chapter in the colourful career of one of the game's most underrated players and of the sport's most successful hustlers." Riggs was featured on the cover of both *Sports Illustrated* and *Time*. Court retired from the sport in 1977.

"I'm like a fire horse when the alarm goes off in a battle against a woman," said Riggs. "Don't ever count me out. Now I want King bad. I'll play her on clay, grass, wood, cement, marble or roller skates. We got to keep this sex thing going. I'm a woman specialist now. I'm going around the world to challenge all the woman champions. England, France, Czechoslovakia, everywhere. Me against them, sex battles. I've found a whole different life."

Four months later, fed up with Riggs's taunts, 29-year-old King accepted the challenge and they played for $100,000 before an audience of 30,472 at the Houston Astrodome, Texas on Thursday, 20 September 1973. The showbiz razzmatazz was in evidence as King made her way onto the court on a litter carried by four bare-chested muscle men (she had yet to come out as lesbian) dressed in the style of ancient slaves, while Riggs was in a rickshaw pulled by a bevy of dolly birds. Riggs gave King a large Sugar Daddy lollipop while she gave him a piglet to represent his male chauvinism. King won in straight sets, 6-4, 6-3, 6-3, although at one point in the first set she was 3-2 down when Riggs broke her serve. According to commentator Jack Kramer, "I don't think Billie Jean played all that well. She hit a lot of short balls which Bobby could have taken advantage of had he been in shape. I would never take anything away from Billie Jean – because she was smart enough to prepare herself properly – but it might have been different if Riggs hadn't kept running around. It was more than one woman who took care of Bobby Riggs in Houston." Approximately 50 million people in America watched the game on TV in America and another 40 million worldwide. Rumours have since circulated that Riggs threw the match to pay off his debts. In 1988, he was diagnosed with prostate cancer. He died from the disease on 25 October 1995.

FIRST

ATP WORLD NO 1 RANKED PLAYER

Ilie Năstase, The Association of Tennis Professionals,
London, England. Thursday, 23 August 1973

The Association of Tennis Professionals (ATP) was founded in September 1972 by Donald Dell, Jack Kramer and Cliff Drysdale, to look after the interests of professional tennis players. Ilie Năstase became the first ATP World No 1 ranked player on August 23, 1973. Pete Sampras spent a total of 286 weeks at the top of the ATP rankings and holds the record of six consecutive years ended as world number one.

FIRST

GRAND SLAM TOURNAMENT WITH

EQUAL MONEY FOR MEN AND WOMEN

US OPEN, WEST SIDE TENNIS CLUB, ONE TENNIS
PLACE, FOREST HILLS, QUEENS, NEW YORK 11375
UNITED STATES OF AMERICA. MONDAY, 27 AUGUST
– SUNDAY, 9 SEPTEMBER 1973

The US Open was held for the 93rd time in late summer 1973. It was the first Grand Slam at which both the winners of the Men's and Women's Singles titles – John Newcombe and Margaret Court – took home the same pay packet $25,000. The first-round losers left with $400 in their pockets. It took 28 years for the Australian Open to follow suit, offering both genders equal prize money in 2001. On 22 February 2007, the All England Club said it would offer men and women the same pay. On 16 March 2007, the French Tennis Federation announced that it would offer equal prize money to men and women. Christian Bimes, the president, said, "It has been our objective since 2005. Last year, the first step was to award equal rewards to the winners of the Men's and Women's Singles. In 2007, the parity will be total."

ONLY
SOVIET PLAYER TO WIN A GRAND SLAM FINAL

ONLY
SOVIET PLAYER TO REACH A WIMBLEDON FINAL

OLGA MOROZOVA, WOMEN'S DOUBLES, FRENCH OPEN, STADE ROLAND-GARROS, 2 AVENUE GORDON BENNETT, 75016 PARIS, FRANCE. JUNE 1974; LADIES' SINGLES, THE CHAMPIONSHIPS, CHURCH ROAD, WIMBLEDON, LONDON SW19 5AE ENGLAND. FRIDAY, 5 JULY 1974

Born on 22 February 1949, Olga Vasilyevna Morozova won the Wimbledon Juniors' Singles title in 1965 when she was 16. In 1968, she and Alex Metreveli were **the first Soviet Union players to reach a Grand Slam final** when they teamed up at Wimbledon, but lost to Margaret Court and Ken Fletcher in the Mixed Doubles final 6-1, 14-12. Two years later, they also lost in the Mixed Doubles final to Rosemary Casals and Ilie Năstase 6-3, 4-6, 9-7. In 1972, Morozova became **the first Soviet player to reach the singles final of a major tournament** when she was the runner-up at the 1972 Italian Open. The peak of her career came in 1974 when she reached the finals of the singles at the French Open and Wimbledon Championships. At the French Open she was seeded number three behind Chris Evert and Virginia Wade. She lost to Evert 6-1, 6-2 on 16 June 1974. She and Evert won the Women's

Doubles Championship, beating Frenchwoman Gail Chanfreau and West German Katja Ebbinghaus 6-4, 2-6, 6-1. At Wimbledon she beat the number one seed Billie Jean King in the quarter-final in straight sets and Virginia Wade in the semi-final but took three sets after Wade won the first 6-1. Evert won the final 6-0, 6-4. In 1977, Morozova retired because of the Soviet policy against South Africa and became a coach. In 1990, she became the Lawn Tennis Association's national coach, based at Bisham Abbey. In 2000, the Russian Tennis Federation named Morozova as the Russian Tennis Player of the 20th century.

FIRST
BLACK PLAYER TO WIN
GENTLEMEN'S SINGLES AT WIMBLEDON

ONLY
PLAYER TO WIN AMATEUR AND OPEN
NATIONAL CHAMPIONSHIPS IN THE SAME YEAR

ONLY
BLACK PLAYER TO WIN SINGLES TITLE
AT WIMBLEDON, US OPEN
AND AUSTRALIAN OPEN

ONLY
US OPEN WON BY ARTHUR ASHE

Arthur Ashe, US Amateur Championships, Longwood Cricket Club, 564 Hammond Street, Chestnut Hill, Massachusetts 02467 United States of America. Sunday, 25 August 1968; US Open, West Side Tennis Club, One Tennis Place, Forest Hills, Queens, New York 11375, United States of America. Sunday, 8 September 1968; Australian Open, White City Stadium, Rushcutters Bay, Sydney, New South Wales 2021, Australia. Tuesday, 27 January 1970; Gentlemen's Singles, The Championships, Church Road, Wimbledon, London SW19 5AE England. Saturday, 5 July 1975

The US Amateur Championships was held for the first time in 1968 and won by Arthur Ashe, then a student at UCLA on a tennis scholarship. He beat Davis Cup team-mate Bob Lutz in a five-set thriller – 4-6, 6-3, 8-10, 6-0, 6-4. The tournament did not take place from 1971 until 1980 but was revived in 1981. In 1995, it became the Intercollegiate Tennis Association Summer Championships. The interest was not really there and it was finally abandoned in 2011.

The same year as Ashe's amateur win, he also won the US Open title – the first black man to do so and the only player to win the amateur and professional titles in the same year. It is a record that now cannot be beaten or equalled. In the first round of the competition, Ashe – seeded number five – received a bye. In the second round, he was paired against 52-year-old Frank Parker, a four-times Grand Slam winner and the oldest man to compete in a Grand Slam singles tournament. Ashe won comfortably in straight sets 6-4, 6-2, 6-2. In the third round, he met Briton Paul Hutchins (achieving his best US Open result) but Ashe sailed through 6-3, 6-4, 6-1. In round four, Ashe beat Australian Roy Emerson, the number 14 seed, in straight sets – 6-4, 9-7, 6-2. In the quarter-final, Ashe was drawn against South African Cliff Drysdale, who was seeded 16. The first set was a marathon with Drysdale winning 10-8. Ashe won the second set with relative ease 6-3 but Drysdale pushed him close in the third set, which Ashe won 9-7. Ashe won the fourth and final set 6-4. In the semi-final, Ashe played his Davis Cup team-mate Clark Graebner, the number seven seed. Graebner took the first set 6-4 and then pushed Ashe hard in the next two, but Ashe won 8-6, 7-5 before a relatively easy 6-2 victory in the fourth set. The match was the subject of the 1969 book *Levels of the Game* by Professor John McPhee of Princeton University. In the final Ashe met Dutchman Tom Okker, who was seeded eight. The number one seed, Rod Laver, had been despatched by Cliff Drysdale in the fourth round. Ashe took the first set in the final 14-12 before Okker won the second 7-5. The third set was a victory for Ashe 6-3 before the fourth and fifth sets went to Okker and then Ashe by the same margin. During the match Ashe served 26 aces.

At UCLA, Ashe had been in the Reserve Officer Training Corps which meant he had to join the army after he graduated. On 4 August 1966, Arthur Ashe reported for duty with the United States Army where, after basic training, he was commissioned as a second lieutenant in the Adjutant General's Corps. He was promoted to first lieutenant on 23 February 1968. Ashe's brother, Johnnie, volunteered to serve an additional tour in Vietnam so that Ashe did not have to put himself in danger. At the US Open prize-giving, Ashe was referred to as "General Ashe" by Robert J. Kelleher, the president of the US Lawn Tennis Association. The press at the time referred to Ashe as "the only Negro male tennis player of world class stature".

"Arthur could beat any player on a given day or he could lose to a bad player if he was mishitting," recalled his Davis Cup captain Donald Dell. "All the elements fell in place. There were a lot of upsets and he just took advantage of the opportunity."

In December 1968, Ashe was part of the victorious American Davis Cup side which beat Australia 4-1 in Adelaide. On 12 December 1968, he became the No 1 ranked US player by the United States Lawn Tennis Association. Ashe was demobbed in 1969. A number of world-class players including Rod Laver, Ken Rosewall, Andrés Gimeno, Pancho Gonzales, Roy Emerson and Fred Stolle were all missing from the 1970 Australian Open because they were all affiliated with the National Tennis League and could not enter the competition because the prizes were not sufficiently big. Arthur Ashe had lost in the 1966 and 1967 finals so was determined to win the prize. He was seeded four and, in the second round, Ashe had a titanic struggle against Australian Geoff Masters, winning the first set 17-15 but easing through the second and third sets 6-2, 6-3. In the third round, another Australian Bill Bowery pushed him but Ashe triumphed 6-3, 9-7, 6-4. In the quarter-final, yet another Australian, the number ten seed Ray Ruffels, took him to four sets but Ashe won 6-8, 6-3, 6-4, 6-2. The semi-final on 26 January 1970 saw more drama as Ashe met American Dennis Ralston, the number six seed. Ashe was leading 2-1 in the fourth set when Ralston was forced to retire with a bad back and Ashe ahead two sets to one – 6-3, 8-10, 6-3. His opponent in the final on 27 January 1970 was number 12 seed Dick

Crealy, another Aussie. Ashe won in straight sets 6-4, 9-7, 6-2. Ashe was the first non-Australian to win the title since Alex Olmedo triumphed over Neale Fraser in 1959.

Ashe had been a semi-finalist at Wimbledon in 1968 and 1969. In 1975, he was the number six seed behind the defending champion Jimmy Connors, Ken Rosewall, Björn Borg, Guillermo Vilas and Ilie Năstase. As the tournament progressed, the seeds dropped – Năstase out in the second round, Rosewall a fourth-round casualty, and Vilas ousted in the quarter-finals. In the first round Ashe beat Bob Hewitt, the first man Connors had played at Wimbledon. In his first match, Connors injured his knee. A physio at Stamford Bridge, the home of Chelsea FC, diagnosed Connors with "hairline fractures" of the shin and recommended rest, but for Connors this was out of the question. In his second match, he beat the Indian Vijay Amritraj and, refusing to show any sign of weakness to any opponent, did not wear any support for his knee or shin. In the third round, Connors beat Cambridge-educated Briton Mark Cox who, at Bournemouth on 24 April 1968, became **the first amateur to beat a professional**, when he defeated Pancho Gonzalez in five sets over two and a quarter hours.

After the weekend rest, Connors and Ashe were both back in action although Connors was summoned before the Wimbledon committee to explain some less than complimentary remarks he made about the state of the grass at the tournament. Ashe beat Borg in the quarter-finals but needed five long sets to prevail against Roche in the semi-finals. Then it was the final and 6ft 1in Ashe was up against the number one seed. Ashe, nearing his 32nd birthday, had never defeated 5ft 10in Connors in three previous meetings. In addition, a few days before Wimbledon fortnight began, Connors issued a writ for slander for $3 million against Ashe for questioning Connors's patriotism. The two men could not have been more different. Ashe wanted to meet Nelson Mandela, Connors wanted to meet Dean Martin. Ashe read a lot, Connors boasted that he had never read a book and had no plans to change the habit of a lifetime. Ashe was the president of the Association of Tennis Professionals, Connors refused to join. But both men were members of London's Playboy Club.

Connors won the toss and elected to serve. Ashe took the first set 6-1. Ashe sliced his backhand low and deep, mixed up his pace, placed lobs effectively and instead of booming big first serves, he sliced his serve wide to both Connors's backhand and forehand and charged the net. Ashe was at 3-0 in the second set when, after winning two points, Connors lost the next one. A voice in the crowd yelled out, "Come on, Jimmy!" Without missing a beat, the younger man looked in the direction of the voice and muttered, "I'm trying, for Chrissakes, I'm trying." BBC commentator Dan Maskell said, "Well, I've never heard that before on Centre Court." Ashe took the second set by the same margin, 6-1. While changing ends, Connors would sit – it was **the first year that chairs had been provided for the players** – and consult a piece of paper he had tucked in his sock. It turned out to be a message from his grandmother. The third set went to Connors 7-5. Ashe was on a roll and he took the fourth set 6-4 and the championship. "I always thought I could win," Ashe said afterwards. "I was pretty confident. I had been playing well." Ashe pocketed £10,000 (£102,500 at 2020 values) for the win and shortly after the tournament, Connors dropped his slander suit against Ashe.

DID YOU KNOW?

Because he was a soldier and he wanted to play in the Davis Cup, Arthur Ashe could not accept the $14,000 first-prize money for winning the US Open in 1968, which was given to runner-up Tom Okker. The championship winner received just $20 each day in expenses. His accommodation was paid for by the US Lawn Tennis Association.

FIRST

NIGHT PLAY IN GRAND SLAM TENNIS

US OPEN, WEST SIDE TENNIS CLUB, ONE TENNIS PLACE, FOREST HILLS, QUEENS, NEW YORK 11375 UNITED STATES OF AMERICA. WEDNESDAY, 2 – SUNDAY, 13 SEPTEMBER 1975

Another change came about at the US Open in 1975. Players had complained that the ball bounced unevenly on the grass courts at the West Side Tennis Club so for the new tournament play was conducted on a green-coloured Har-Tru clay surface, a surface slightly harder and faster than red clay. The competition also brought in floodlights to enable matches to be played at night. The announcement for night play was made on 19 July 1975 and on eight of the 12 days, play took place after dark with the courts illuminated with 150-feet high floodlights at a cost of $100,000.

FIRST

TENNIS PLAYER TO WIN
BBC OVERSEAS
SPORTS PERSONALITY OF THE YEAR

Arthur Ashe, BBC Television Theatre, London, England.
Wednesday, 10 December 1975

The Overseas Personality award was first presented in 1960, six years after the BBC Sports Personality of the Year award was introduced. Five months after winning Wimbledon, Arthur Ashe won the BBC Overseas Sports Personality of the Year, the first tennis player to be awarded the honour. The programme was hosted by Frank Bough and Harry Carpenter. Since Ashe won the trophy, a number of tennis players have won: 1979 Björn Borg, 1981 Chris Evert, 1982 Jimmy Connors, 1985 Boris Becker, 1987 Martina Navratilova, 1988 Steffi Graf, 1992 Andre Agassi, 1997 Martina Hingis, 2001 Goran Ivanišević, 2004, 2006, 2007, 2017 Roger Federer, 2010 Rafael Nadal and 2011 Novak Djokovic.

TENNIS TALK

"Let's see what you've got, big boy."

"Hair."

Andre Agassi is bested by Andy Roddick

LAST

AUSTRALIAN TO WIN AUSTRALIAN OPEN MEN'S SINGLES

Mark Edmondson, Men's Singles, Australian Open, Kooyong Lawn
Tennis Club, 489 Glenferrie Road, Kooyong, Victoria 3144, Australia.
Sunday, 4 January 1976

Mark Edmondson was ranked 212 in the world when he entered the
1976 Australian Open. He had been working as a caretaker and general
handyman to supplement his tennis income. Edmondson shocked the
tennis world when he beat defending champion John Newcombe 6-7,
6-3, 7-6, 6-1 in the two-and-a-half hour final. The match was delayed
for 30 minutes because of bad weather, which included 45mph winds
and a temperature that dropped from 104°F to 79°F in five minutes.
Edmondson said, "I'm suffering from shock and exhilaration. I think I
might have a couple of bottles of bubbly tonight." He is still the lowest-
ranked player to have won a Grand Slam tournament since the rankings
were introduced in 1973. The Australian Open Men's Singles was
Edmondson's only career Grand Slam singles title.

ONLY

MAJOR FINAL THAT TOOK THREE MONTHS TO COMPLETE

Men's Doubles final, Italian Open, Foro Italico, Rome, Italy. Sunday,
30 May 1976; the Woodlands Inn, 2301 Millbend Drive, Texas 77380,
United States of America. Wednesday, 15 September 1976

American Brian Gottfried and Mexican Raúl Ramírez got through to
the final of the Italian Open, where they faced the Australian pair of
Geoff Masters and John Newcombe. The first set went to Gottfried
and Ramírez 7-6 on a tie-break but the Australians won the second set

7-5. The third and fourth sets both ended 6-3, third to Gottfried and Ramírez and the fourth to the Australians. And then it got dark and the umpire took the players off for bad light, which is where the problem started. Each of the players had other commitments, which meant that final had to be completed not only in a different venue but a different city, a different country and a different continent. The players resumed their final at the Grow Professionals Doubles Championships, Houston, Texas on 15 September – 108 days after the match was suspended for bad light. Gottfried and Ramírez won the fifth set 6-3 to take the title.

FIRST
BALL GIRLS AT WIMBLEDON
THE CHAMPIONSHIPS, CHURCH ROAD, WIMBLEDON, LONDON SW19 5AE ENGLAND. 20 JUNE – 2 JULY 1977

As much a tradition at Wimbledon as strawberries and cream, Robinsons Barley Water and John McEnroe losing his temper, the ball boys collect and deliver balls to players, hand them towels and even hold umbrellas over them if it is too hot. One was even asked to peel a banana for a player in January 2020. Rafa Nadal once handed an energy bar wrapper to a ball boy to place in a nearby bin instead of doing it himself. The BBGs, as they are known, "should not be seen. They should blend into the background and get on with their jobs quietly." That is the official view. From 1920, the Wimbledon ball boys were provided by the Shaftesbury Children's Home, a charity set up in the 19th century to support young people in care. They wore a uniform of a grey shirt, dark short trousers and dark socks. From 1946 until 1966, the Dr Barnardo's home in Hertfordshire, Goldings, began supplying them. Only a third of the boys who applied were successful. They were trained by the Reverend Mr E. Appleyard. Each day of the tournament they were woken at 6am by a bugle to ensure they were ready for the two-and-a-half hour journey by coach to the ground. From 1947 until 1954, they wore grey shirts and long, dark trousers. In 1955, 1956 and 1957, they wore a shirt in the club colours of purple and green and long, dark trousers. From 1958 until 2004, they donned shirts and shorts in the club colours. A new kit was introduced in 2006 designed by Polo Ralph Lauren.

After two more years of the Shaftesbury Children's Home providing the ball boys, in 1967 and 1968, Wimbledon began using boys from schools in the Merton and Wandsworth area in 1969. In 1977, the first ball girls appeared at Wimbledon, chosen from local schools. Three years later, ball boys and ball girls began servicing the same matches. The first ball girls did not appear on Centre Court until 1985. For those selected to work at The Championships, training begins in February of each year.

LAST
ENGLISH PLAYER TO WIN
WIMBLEDON LADIES' SINGLES
VIRGINIA WADE, LADIES' SINGLES, THE CHAMPIONSHIPS, CHURCH ROAD, WIMBLEDON, LONDON SW19 5AE ENGLAND. FRIDAY, 1 JULY 1977

Sarah Virginia Wade was born in Bournemouth on 10 July 1945 (the same day as iconic sports commentator John Motson). In 1977, Wade made her 16th appearance at the Wimbledon Championships and reached the final, the only time she would go that far. She was a semi-finalist in 1974, 1976 and 1978 and reached the quarter-finals on six other occasions; 1977 was the centenary year of The Championships and also the Silver Jubilee of HM the Queen – and the monarch attended Wimbledon for the first time since 1962 to watch the final. Wade was seeded number three behind the defending champion Chris Evert and Martina Navratilova and ahead of Sue Barker. This was **the first time Wimbledon seeded more than eight players for the Ladies' Singles title**. For 1977 only, there were 12, then the number increased to 16 in 1978. In the first round, Wade was drawn against wild card entrant Jo Durie and saw off her fellow Briton 6-2, 6-2. Round two saw her beat American Betsy Nagelsen 6-2, 6-1. In the third round she defeated South African

Yvonne Vermaak 6-1, 6-2. Her fourth-round opponent was the future Mrs Björn Borg, Mariana Simionescu from Romania. Wade won 9-7, 6-3 to progress to the quarter-final. There she met the American Rosie Casals and saw off the number six seed 7-5, 6-2. The semi-finalists were Wade, Dutchwoman Betty Stöve, Chris Evert and Sue Barker, leading to the possibility of an all-British final for the first time since 1961, when Angela Mortimer had defeated Christine Truman 4-6, 6-4, 7-5. It was not to be – Wade beat Evert in three sets 6-2, 4-6, 6-1 but Barker was unable to see off Stöve losing 6-4, 2-6, 6-4. It would be Barker's best showing at The Championships.

For the final, Wade, 31, arrived on court wearing a pink cardigan over her whites. Stöve took the first set 6-4 but Wade rallied and took the next two sets 6-3, 6-1. "Winning Wimbledon was the thing that made my career worthwhile," Wade said. After the Queen presented the trophy the crowd broke out into a rendition of "For She's a Jolly Good Fellow". Thirty years after her victory, Wade commented, "Angela Mortimer had won in 1961 and Ann Jones in 1969, so when I won in 1977 we all thought it happened every eight years, but maybe we were just anomalies, because there was Sue Barker and Jo Durie, but then the [British] players just petered out." In 1989, Wade was inducted into the International Tennis Hall of Fame.

FIRST
TRANSSEXUAL PLAYER IN THE US OPEN
ONLY
PLAYER TO HAVE COMPETED IN BOTH
THE MEN'S AND WOMEN'S SINGLES
AT GRAND SLAM LEVEL

RENEE RICHARDS, UNITED STATES NATIONAL CHAMPIONSHIPS, WEST SIDE TENNIS CLUB, 1 TENNIS PLACE, FOREST HILLS, NEW YORK 11375 UNITED STATES OF AMERICA. SATURDAY,

29 AUGUST 1953; US OPEN, WEST SIDE TENNIS CLUB, 1 TENNIS PLACE, FOREST HILLS, NEW YORK 11375 UNITED STATES OF AMERICA. THURSDAY, 1 SEPTEMBER 1977

Born in 1934, the son of an orthopaedic surgeon and one of the first female psychiatrists in America, Richard Raskind grew up "a nice Jewish boy" in Forest Hills, Queens. He became an ophthalmologist and later joined the US Navy. He played in the US Open for the first time in 1953 and was knocked out in the first round. By the time Dick was a teenager, he was, on his own initiative, shaving his legs and cross-dressing. At college, he began calling himself Renee. At the time he was uncertain of his sexuality and became depressed and suicidal. In June 1970, he married Barbara Mole, a model, and fathered a son, Nicholas, in 1972. They divorced in 1975, the year he had gender reassignment surgery.

In 1976, Richards applied to the US Open to play as a woman but was refused. Richards then sued the United States Tennis Association, the body that oversees the US Open, in New York in 1977, winning the case on 16 August 1977. Participating in the competition, Richards was drawn in the first round against Briton Virginia Wade, the number three seed. Asked how she would feel if she lost to Richards, Wade said, "I'd demand that she be tested." Wade said she was joking and was misquoted, but did admit she was not "comfortable with the whole idea". By the time the match started before a capacity stadium crowd of 12,921, Richards and Wade were not on speaking terms. Wade ran out the victor easily 6-1, 6-4 in one hour and one minute.

Richards played professionally from 1977 to 1981 and later said that living as a man had given her unfair advantages over women, adding, "Having lived for the past 30 years, I know if I'd had surgery at the age of 22, and then at 24 went on the tour, no genetic woman in the world would have been able to come close to me. And so, I've reconsidered my opinion." In March 2019, Richards said, "I would have been mortified if I had won Grand Slams as a woman, and I would have stopped on the spot. I would never have pursued something that would have given me an unfair advantage. But I wasn't any more successful than I had been when I had been competing in 35-and-over tournaments as a man before

I had the sex change. I was a finalist in the US Open 35-and-over, just as I was in the final of the women's 35-and-over many years later. I was a good player and entitled to win matches, but if I had overwhelmed the field, of course not. It would have been crazy."

LAST
US OPEN AT FOREST HILLS

**US Open, West Side Tennis Club, One Tennis Place,
Forest Hills, New York 11375 United States of America.
Sunday, 11 September 1977**

The US Open was held at the West Side Tennis Club for the first time in 1915. It stayed there until 1920 and then returned in 1924 where it stayed until 1977. Despite a number of innovations occurring at Forest Hills in the New York borough of Queens, including the introduction of seedings in 1927, tie-breakers in 1970, equal prize money for men and women in 1973, and night play in 1975, the US Tennis Association decided that the area was too congested and the club management too old-fashioned to host America's prime tennis tournament. Plans were made to build a stadium in Flushing Meadows, the site of the New York's World's Fairs in 1939–1940 and 1964–1965. Ground was broken on the new site on 6 October 1977 in a ceremony reduced to five minutes because of rain. The Men's Singles final was the last US Open match played at Forest Hills and was contested by Jimmy Connors and Guillermo Vilas. Vilas lost just 16 games in five matches leading up to the semi-final. In the final he beat Connors 2-6, 6-3, 7-6 (7-4), 6-0 to win his second Grand Slam title and his only US Open title. He was **the first Argentine to win the US Open**. Many of the sell-out 16,000 crowd were Latinos who cheered for the Argentine. When he won, they invaded the court and hoisted him shoulder high to parade around the horseshoe-shaped stadium. Connors was so annoyed by losing and the subsequent court invasion, he did not stay for the trophy presentation.

Without the US Open, West Side fell into a state of disrepair and in 2010 an offer was made to knock it down and build homes on the site. By 2011, it was described as a "crumbling ruin". The New York City Landmarks Preservation Commission refused to award the stadium landmark status. In mid-2013, however, the stadium re-opened as an outdoor music venue with Mumford & Sons performing the first concert.

━━◆━

ONLY

PLAYER TO WIN US OPEN ON
THREE DIFFERENT SURFACES

Jimmy Connors, Men's Singles, US Open, v Ken Rosewall, West Side Tennis Club, 1 Tennis Place, Forest Hills, New York 11375 United States of America. Sunday, 8 September 1974; Men's Singles, US Open, v Björn Borg, West Side Tennis Club, 1 Tennis Place, Forest Hills, New York 11375 United States of America. Sunday, 12 September 1976; Men's Singles, US Open, v Björn Borg, USTA National Tennis Center, Flushing Meadows-Corona Park, Flushing, New York 11368, United States of America. Sunday, 10 September 1978

━━◆━

In 1974, the number one seed Jimmy Connors won his first US Open title, beating Ken Rosewall 6-1, 6-0, 6-1 on grass. It created a record as the shortest Grand Slam Men's Singles final, both in number of games and duration, taking only one hour and 18 minutes to finish. Two years later, he bested Björn Borg 6-4, 3-6, 7-6 (11-9), 6-4 in four sets on clay (clay Har-Tru). Connors won despite scoring fewer points in total (121) than the Swede (123). In 1978, the first time the tournament was played on the new hard deco court surface and also the first time since 1915 it was not played at the West Side Tennis Club venue in Forest Hills, Connors again beat Borg 6-4, 6-2, 6-2. He also won at Flushing Meadows on 12 September 1982 and 11 September 1983 on the hard court surface.

TENNIS TALK

"I always felt like an outsider. Then, as I got older, I deliberately kept myself in that same mode because it gave me an edge. I might have dipped a toe on the inside, but really I was always better on my own."

Jimmy Connors, May 2013

ONLY

GRAND SLAM WINNER TO
MARRY A PLAYBOY PLAYMATE

JIMMY CONNORS, UNITED STATES OF
AMERICA, 1979

Hugh Hefner launched *Playboy*, his iconic magazine, in December 1953 (he originally intended to call it Stag Party) and Marilyn Monroe was the first centrefold. A year and two months before the magazine was launched, James Scott Connors was born at East St Louis, Illinois. He was 19 when he spotted 17-year-old Chris Evert in the dining room at Queen's Club. Despite the fact that Evert – who had been raised a good Catholic girl and wore a crucifix round her neck on court – was being chaperoned by her formidable mother Colette, he sat down beside her. Connors arranged to take her out to dinner later that week and their first date finished at the Playboy Club. In 1974, Connors and Evert became engaged. That year, both won their individual singles' titles at Wimbledon and at the Champions' Dinner they danced to "The Girl That I Marry". They intended to tie the knot that November, but broke off their engagement the month before. "We were entirely too young to get married," Evert said. "We hadn't had any life experiences. We would never have seen each other. It was more important to both of us to try to be number one in the world rather than to sacrifice for each other. It would never have worked, but we have had a great relationship through the years."

In 1979, she read an interview with British Davis Cup player John Lloyd. He spoke of the loneliness of the globetrotting professional athlete. She arranged for a girlfriend to ask him to go dancing with them at Tramp, the London nightclub. "That was our first date and we hit it off," she said later. On 17 April 1979, they married. However, what she saw as his lack of ambition frustrated her and she began an affair with the singer Adam Faith. This led to a separation in 1983 but the couple got back together and chronicled their marriage in a biography entitled *Lloyd On Lloyd*, which was co-authored by the then prime minister's daughter

Carol Thatcher. However, the marriage did not last and they divorced in 1987. "Both my parents were really sad and disappointed," Evert once said. "My mum wrote me a letter. My dad didn't talk to me. It was because my dad wasn't talking to me that Martina [Navratilova] invited me to Aspen." At a New Year's party at the ski resort's Hotel Jerome, Evert met Andy Mill, a former downhill racer with the US ski team. He sat next to her and asked: "What are you doing here?" She said that she was in Aspen to ski and the next day he helped her down the mountain by skiing backwards the whole way holding her hands. They married in 1988 and had three sons: Alexander (b. 1991), Nicholas (b. 1994) and Colton (b. 1996). On 13 November 2006, Evert filed for divorce from Mill, the divorce becoming final on 4 December 2006. Evert is said to have paid Mill $7m in a settlement. On 28 June 2008, in the Bahamas, she married Australian golfer Greg Norman. They separated on 2 October 2009 and divorced on 8 December 2009.

In November 1976, 25-year-old brunette Patti McGuire graced *Playboy*'s centre spread with pictures by Pompeo Posar. So taken by her were they, the magazine's editors named her the 1977 Playmate of the Year. In 1979, she married Jimmy Connors. They have two children, a son Brett and a daughter Aubree. In his autobiography published in 2013, Connors revealed that he found it hard to remain faithful. After he had cheated on McGuire early in their marriage, she began divorce proceedings, but later she forgave Connors and has been with him ever since. "Bottom line is I loved him," McGuire said. "I loved him. I came from a broken family. My mother and father were divorced when I was 19 months old. No one's infallible. We all make mistakes, and there is one word that is in the vocabulary, everyone who gets through life has to use, it's called forgiveness."

"I consider myself lucky to have ended up with just the one woman," Connors said. "Tennis gave me everything I became but I needed a woman who could handle all that. I've been married to Patti for [41] years, and she's stayed with me through the ups and the downs. I was great at confrontation on the court but not so much off it. Rather than confront issues, I would let things slide and go into the dark place in my head. Now I'm so grateful that my family stuck by me throughout all that."

In the book, which was published in the United States on 14 May 2013, Connors strongly hinted – without stating it – that Evert had had an abortion, against his wishes, just before they were due to be married. He wrote, "An issue had arisen as a result of youthful passion, and a decision had to be made as a couple. Chrissie called to say she was coming out to LA to take care of the 'issue'. I was perfectly happy to let nature take its course and accept responsibility for what was to come. Chrissie, however, had already made up her mind that the timing was bad and too much was riding on her future. She asked me to handle the details." Evert said: "I am extremely disappointed that he used the book to misrepresent a private matter that took place 40 years ago, and made it public without my knowledge." Connors responded: "It was a part of my life. At the time, a very important part of my life. It's a book about my life and it was very subtle. There are 400 other pages in the book, but everyone focuses on that one."

TENNIS TALK

"I remember when Jimmy and I went into confession and he came out a half-hour later and I said, 'How'd it go?' He said, 'I wasn't finished. The priest said come back next Sunday.'"

Chris Evert on Jimmy Connors

ONLY

PLAYER AT WIMBLEDON TO
SHOW HER NIPPLES
ON CENTRE COURT

Linda Siegel, Ladies' Singles, The Championships, Church Road, Wimbledon, London SW19 5AE England. Thursday, 28 June 1979

Linda Siegel was 18 years old when she was drawn to play against Billie Jean King in the second round of the Ladies' Singles having received a bye in the first round. She lost in straight sets to seventh-seed King 6-1, 6-3, but it was her dress that made headlines. Backless, she did not wear a bra and as a result fell out of the dress a couple of times. King said, "That's great if she's happy. The audience sure was happy. If you're well-endowed you might as well show it." Siegel never played at Wimbledon again.

FIRST

"RETIREMENT" BY CHRIS EVERT

CHRIS EVERT, UNITED STATES OF AMERICA. WEDNESDAY, 30 JANUARY 1980

Announcing that "I don't enjoy winning, and I don't enjoy losing. I just don't enjoy playing anymore," Chris Evert announced she was retiring from tennis at the age of 25. The retirement lasted just three months before Evert returned to professional tennis.

FIRST

USE OF CYCLOPS AT WIMBLEDON

THE CHAMPIONSHIPS, CHURCH ROAD, WIMBLEDON, LONDON SW19 5AE
ENGLAND. MONDAY, 23 JUNE - SATURDAY, 5 JULY 1980

Many sports have electronic devices to help umpires, judges and referees in making the correct decision for points, goals, wickets, etc. In 1980, Cyclops was introduced to Centre Court, Court Number One and Court Number Two at the Wimbledon Championships to make close service-line calls. It works by transmitting infra-red rays a little over three eighths of an inch above the court. It makes a loud beep when the ball breaks the beams. Initially, only the line judge could hear the beep through headphones but it was later decided to broadcast the beep to the entire crowd. In 1981, the US Open began to use Cyclops. In 2007, Cyclops was replaced by Hawk-Eye – the high-speed multi-camera technology which tracks the trajectory of a moving ball and is used in international cricket. The Sony-owned (since March 2011) Hawk-Eye system was developed in the United Kingdom by Paul Hawkins.

DID YOU KNOW?

Cyclops was invented by Bill Carlton, a former aircraft engineer, who also invented the plastic shuttlecock.

ONLY

MAN TO WIN WIMBLEDON
AND THE FRENCH OPEN CHAMPIONSHIPS
IN THE SAME THREE CONSECUTIVE YEARS

Björn Borg, v Jimmy Connors, Gentlemen's Singles, the Championships, Church Road, Wimbledon, London. SW19 5AE England. Saturday, 8 July 1978; v Roscoe Tanner, Gentlemen's Singles, The Championships, Church Road, Wimbledon, London. SW19 5AE England. Saturday, 7 July 1979; v John McEnroe, Gentlemen's Singles, The Championships, Church Road, Wimbledon, London SW19 5AE England. Saturday, 5 July 1980; French Open v Guillermo Vilas, Men's Singles, Stade Roland-Garros, 2 Avenue Gordon Bennett, 75016 Paris, France. Sunday, 11 June 1978; v Víctor Pecci, Sr, Men's Singles, Stade Roland-Garros, 2 Avenue Gordon Bennett, 75016 Paris, France. Sunday, 10 June 1979; v Vitas Gerulaitis, Men's Singles, Stade Roland-Garros, 2 Avenue Gordon Bennett, 75016 Paris, France. Sunday, 8 June 1980

Swede Björn Borg won his first Wimbledon title in 1976 and did not lose a match at the tournament until the final in 1981, when John McEnroe beat him. In 1978, in a repeat of the previous year's final, Borg successfully defended his title, easily beating Jimmy Connors 6-2, 6-2, 6-3 in one hour and 49 minutes. The following year, Borg beat another American when he defeated Roscoe Tanner 6-7 (4-7), 6-1, 3-6, 6-3, 6-4 in two hours and 49 minutes. Borg came back from two sets to one down to win his fourth consecutive Wimbledon and "the toughest match I have played here". Borg added, "I always felt that I was one step behind Roscoe, even when I was a break ahead of him in the fifth set. I always was a little behind because he was serving so well. I had so many problems to break his serve."

Tanner commented, "You've got to take chances against Björn. You can't go out and just play careful tennis because he's better than anybody else at that type of game. You've got to take some chances on his second serve, mix up your service and keep him from getting into a groove. If you play just a steady, hard-hitting game, he likes that. You've got to do some things to break up his rhythm, take some gambles, go for your shots all the time. You can't worry if you miss some because if you stop staying back and playing his game you're going to get beaten for sure."

In 1980, Borg won his fifth Wimbledon title in a row. He beat his rival John McEnroe in the final, 1-6, 7-5, 6-3, 6-7 (16-18), 8-6 in three hours and 53 minutes. The final was made into a film titled *Borg vs McEnroe*.

At Roland-Garros in 1978, Borg beat Argentinian Guillermo Vilas, 6-1, 6-1, 6-3. It was Borg's fifth career Grand Slam title, and his third French Open title. Vilas said, "He played so well, he didn't give me any chances at all. I knew if I was going to play from the baseline all the time, I was going to win more games but not the match. So, I tried different tactics but it did not work. Nothing worked." A year later, Borg won his seventh career Grand Slam title and his fourth French Open title when he beat the unseeded Paraguayan Víctor Pecci, Sr 6-3, 6-1, 6-7 (6-8), 6-4. Borg said, "I thought I had the match in my hand at 5-2 in the third, but then he started playing better, taking more chances, and I missed a few passing shots. Suddenly, it was five-all. I got to be a little bit scared. I wasn't hitting through my shots and started hitting short, and then he was coming in on every point. He made this the toughest final I have played here." Borg returned 100 out of 107 first serves and lost just 15 points in his first 13 service games. In 1980 in Paris, Borg met Vitas Gerulaitis and won 6-4, 6-1, 6-2. It was the Swede's ninth career Grand Slam title, and his fifth French Open title. Henri Cochet, 79, and one of the Four Musketeers, presented Borg with the trophy. Apart from Borg, Cochet is the only man to have won four French Men's Singles titles. As he handed over the trophy, Cochet did not appear too content that his record had been broken. Said Borg, "He didn't look too happy. He didn't say anything, really. Just 'Well done'. That's all."

TENNIS TALK

"I'll chase that son of a bitch to the ends of the earth to beat him."

Jimmy Connors on Björn Borg, 8 July 1978

DID YOU KNOW?

Wimbledon champion Fred Perry worked as an expert summariser for BBC Radio during the Wimbledon fortnight. Delivered with an American accent and English irony, his comments caused up to 60 letters a day to be sent in by listeners in the 1980s and 1990s. In the Borg–McEnroe final of 1980, which took four and a half hours, Perry claimed that if the time taken between each point and for changing ends had been akin to his day, the match would have been over in one and three-quarter hours.

FIRST

PLAYER TO GET A PUBLIC
WARNING AT WIMBLEDON

JOHN MCENROE, GENTLEMEN'S SINGLES, THE
CHAMPIONSHIPS, CHURCH ROAD, WIMBLEDON, LONDON SW19
5AE ENGLAND. FRIDAY, 4 JULY 1980

The bad boy of tennis John McEnroe thought he had served an ace during his 1980 Wimbledon semi-final against Jimmy Connors, the number three seed. A line judge called the ball out and number two seed McEnroe disagreed. He shouted to the umpire, Pat Smyth: "I am not going to play until you get the referee out here. I want the referee right now." Mr Smyth gave him a public warning, the first ever issued on Centre Court. McEnroe began to walk off the court as the crowd slow handclapped. The tournament referee ordered the point to be replayed. At the end of the game, which McEnroe won 6-3, 3-6, 6-3, 6-4, Connors went over to McEnroe and said: "Don't start anything. Shut your mouth. Just play the match, son. My little boy behaves better than you do. You are both the same age."

FIRST

BROTHER AND SISTER TO WIN
MIXED DOUBLES AT WIMBLEDON

John Austin and Tracy Austin, Mixed Doubles, The Championships, Church Road, Wimbledon, London SW19 5AE England. Saturday, 5 July 1980

Tracy Austin first came to public attention aged 14 when she lost in the quarter-finals of the 1977 US Open to Betty Stöve. By the time she was 21, Austin's playing career was over. In that brief period, she won the US Open twice, beating Chris Evert in 1979 and Martina Navratilova in 1981. The year before, with elder brother John, she won the Wimbledon Mixed Doubles Championship, beating Australians Dianne Fromholtz and Mark Edmondson 4-6, 7-6 (8-6), 6-3. The unseeded Austins won the competition at the third attempt, becoming the first brother and sister, as well as the first American pair since 1956. They beat four seeded pairs and, in the final, came back from going one set and three match points down to beat the Australian duo. Austin, who was only 5ft 4in, was the number two seed that year in the Ladies' Singles but lost in the semi-final to Evonne Cawley. In 1992, she became the youngest person to be inducted into the International Tennis Hall of Fame.

FIRST

FEMALE WIMBLEDON CHAMPION TO COME OUT AS GAY

FIRST

WIMBLEDON CHAMPION SUED FOR PALIMONY

BILLIE JEAN KING, UNITED STATES OF AMERICA. FRIDAY, 1 MAY 1981

Born on 22 November 1943, Billie Jean Moffitt met Larry King in the library at California State University, Los Angeles, where he was majoring in biochemistry and she in history. "He was so gorgeous," she said. They became engaged in the autumn of 1964. The following year on 17 September, they were married at Long Beach, California. She would say that she "was totally in love with Larry" when they tied the knot. It was her husband who introduced her to feminism and encouraged her to play tennis.

In 1968 she became aware of not-so-latent lesbian feelings. In May 1972, she met Beverly Hills hairdresser Marilyn Barnett (born 28 January 1948 as Marilyn Kathryn McRae). They met again not long after and began to spend time together, with King being relieved to spend time with someone not involved with tennis and with whom she could chitchat about inconsequential matters. King then hired Barnett as her secretary-Girl Friday and she was paid $600 each month. In the spring of 1974, King decided that she would have to let Barnett go but agreed severance pay and let her stay at the Malibu beach house for $120 a month rent. After a while, Barnett stopped paying rent and King foolishly did not chase up the situation. In 1977, the two women began to see more of each other but not in a sexual way. In August 1978, King and Barnett clashed in the Kings' New York flat. King asked Barnett to leave the

Malibu beach house. The women had kept their relationship hidden as they believed the public was not ready for an openly gay sportswoman; it therefore came as a shock when Barnett sued Billie Jean for palimony on 1 May 1981. King was forced out of the closet but in a damage-limitation attempt she called the relationship a "fling" and a mistake.

Larry stayed resolutely by her side but the affair was said to have cost her almost $2 million in lost endorsements and meant that she had to carry on playing to pay her bills when her intention had been to retire. Of her sexuality, Billie Jean said, "I wanted to tell the truth but my parents were homophobic and I was in the closet. As well as that, I had people tell me that if I talked about what I was going through, it would be the end of the women's tour. I couldn't get a closet deep enough. One of my big goals was always to be honest with my parents and I couldn't be for a long time. I tried to bring up the subject but felt I couldn't. My mother would say, 'We're not talking about things like that', and I was pretty easily stopped because I was reluctant anyway. I ended up with an eating disorder that came from trying to numb myself from my feelings. I needed to surrender far sooner than I did. At the age of 51, I was finally able to talk about it properly with my parents and no longer did I have to measure my words with them. That was a turning point for me as it meant I didn't have regrets anymore."

The Kings stayed together but divorced in 1987 when Billie Jean fell in love with her doubles partner Ilana Kloss, a relationship that continues to this day. Larry subsequently remarried and Billie Jean is godmother to his son. The story of the affair and aftermath was told in the film *Battle of the Sexes*, which starred Emma Stone as King and Andrea Riseborough as Barnett. At the time, there was no legal protection for lesbian couples.

The original palimony case had been brought in 1971 by Michelle Triola against the actor Lee Marvin, with whom she lived from 1965 to 1970. In 1979, the court ordered Marvin to pay Triola $104,000 but the award was overturned in 1981. From 1976 until her death from lung cancer on 30 October 2009, she lived with the actor Dick Van Dyke. Barnett lost her case against King. In 1981, Barnett attempted suicide and was left paralysed from the waist down.

FIRST

TIME JOHN MCENROE SHOUTED "YOU CANNOT BE SERIOUS"

GENTLEMEN'S SINGLES, THE CHAMPIONSHIPS, CHURCH ROAD,
WIMBLEDON, LONDON SW19 5AE ENGLAND. MONDAY, 22 JUNE 1981

The volatile John McEnroe was born at Wiesbaden, West Germany on 16 February 1959. The tabloids had nicknamed him "Superbrat" and his performances in England in 1981 did nothing to make the fourth estate think they had made an error or misjudgement. Before Wimbledon, he had thrown a tantrum at Queen's Club and then been less than charming in his remarks to the media. In the first round at Wimbledon, the second seeded McEnroe was drawn against fellow American Tom Gullikson, the left-handed brother of Tim, on Number One Court. In the second-set, with the score at one game each and McEnroe leading 30-15, he served. It was called out by the umpire and McEnroe stood looking at the umpire, disbelievingly. Then he lost his temper. He called out to the umpire Edward James of Llanelli, "Chalk came up all over the place, you can't be serious man. You cannot be serious. That ball was on the line. Chalk flew up, it was clearly in, how can you possibly call that out? How many are you going to miss? He's walking over. Everybody knows it's in in the whole stadium and you call it out? Explain that to me, will ya?" Mr James replied, "The linesman called a fault because the ball was on his side of the court ..."

"The chalk came up, it doesn't matter," interrupted McEnroe.

"No, no, the very fact that there is a spread of chalk, as you can see, Mr McEnroe. Your second service." When another call did not go McEnroe's way, he shouted, "You guys are the absolute pits of the world, you know that?" The balding, bespectacled Mr James calmly said, "I'm going to award a point against you Mr McEnroe," to cheers from the crowd before the American called for the referee, Fred Hoyles. Mr James said that the point was "for abusing me and unsportsmanlike behaviour". When Mr Hoyles arrived on court, McEnroe told Mr James to say what he had said. "Tell him what I said. You can repeat it, you can repeat it. It wasn't anything. We're not going to have a point taken away because this guy's an incompetent fool, you know that? That's what he is," said McEnroe to Mr Hoyles.

Later, the referee was again summoned when McEnroe smashed his racquet into the turf. "You are misusing your racquet, Mr McEnroe," said Mr James, to which the blue-headband-wearing player responded, "You are an incompetent fool, an offence against the world," and he was docked another point. The crowd responded with a slow handclap. Gullikson was unimpressed. He said at the time, "It has no place. Everyone's afraid of these guys. All it would take is one default to put them in line. If it was the 120th player in the world they would have defaulted him."

McEnroe won the match in straight sets 7-6, 7-5, 6-3. He commented, "I was just jittery today. The guy did a lousy job but I should not have said what I did. I worry about how I act. I have no one to blame but myself. Others accept bad decisions and so should I. If we do a lousy job, we lose. If they do a lousy job, they should be changed. There were at least eight really bad calls out there. Mind you, with guys like me around, who would want to be an umpire?"

LAST
TIME BOTH FINALISTS IN GENTLEMEN'S SINGLES AT WIMBLEDON USED A WOODEN RACQUET

LAST
WIMBLEDON MATCH
FOR BJÖRN BORG

GENTLEMEN'S SINGLES, THE CHAMPIONSHIPS, CHURCH ROAD, WIMBLEDON, LONDON SW19 5AE ENGLAND. SATURDAY, 4 JULY 1981 2PM

The last time both Gentlemen's Singles finalists at Wimbledon used wooden racquets was the day number one seed Björn Borg was playing number two seed John McEnroe and attempting to equal Willie

Renshaw's six consecutive Gentlemen's Singles titles and Roy Emerson's twelve Grand Slam titles. In the first round the icy Swede had been drawn against American Peter Rennert and had gone through in straight sets 7-6, 6-3, 6-1. Borg easily overcame American Mel Purcell in the second round 6-4, 6-1, 6-3. In the third round, he beat Rolf Gehring from West Germany 6-4, 7-5, 6-0. In the fourth round he came up against another seeded player for the first time when he met the number 16 seed, American Vitas Gerulaitis, and won 7-6, 7-5, 7-6. In the quarter-final, Borg beat the number 12 seed Australian Peter McNamara 7-6, 6-2, 6-3. Borg faced a tough semi-final against Jimmy Connors, the number three seed. Connors smashed Borg 6-0 and won the second set 6-4. Then Borg began his fightback going from two sets down to win the final three 6-3, 6-0, 6-4. John McEnroe met Tom Gullikson in the first round (see above). In the second round, he played Raúl Ramírez of Mexico and won 6-3, 6-7, 6-3, 7-6. In the third round, McEnroe beat his fellow American Bob Lutz 6-4, 6-2, 6-0. His fourth-round opponent was Stan Smith, another American who McEnroe beat 7-5, 3-6, 6-1, 6-2. In the quarter-final, McEnroe was drawn against South African Johan Kriek, who he beat in straight sets 6-1, 7-5, 6-1. Australian Rod Frawley was his opposite number in the semis and McEnroe again lost his temper. He mumbled to himself throughout and stared at the linesmen every time a decision looked even remotely close. In the tenth game, he lost it when umpire Wing Commander George Grimes overruled a call at 5-4 and deuce. "I get screwed by the umpires in this place," he screamed and was promptly given an official warning while the crowd again began a slow handclap. McEnroe won the first set 7-6 and the second 6-4. With the score at 4-4 in the third set, there was another line call that McEnroe disputed. His appeal went nowhere as Wing Commander Grimes upheld the call. McEnroe was now losing 5-4. "You're a disgrace to mankind," yelled McEnroe. The Wing Commander announced a one-point penalty for "unsportsmanlike conduct". McEnroe pleaded with the umpire that he was not addressing the chair. "I was not talking to you, umpire. I was talking to myself. I would like the referee called before you announce the score. What did I say? Please tell me." Fred Hoyles was again summoned. He listened to McEnroe but backed the umpire.

DID YOU KNOW?

It is a tradition that the winners of Wimbledon are made honorary members of the All England Club. In 1981, that honour was not extended to John McEnroe. He then boycotted the Champions' Dinner and missed the opportunity to dance with the Ladies' Champion Chris Evert, who had won her third and last Wimbledon. McEnroe was given membership a year later.

As the arguments flared, the visitor in the Royal Box was diplomatically removed. It was just 25 days before Lady Diana Spencer was due to marry the Prince of Wales. She was sitting with her friend Liz Cooper and ex-King Constantine of Greece. Other VIPs watching the unravelling were the Duchess of Gloucester, Princess Michael of Kent and Foreign Secretary Lord Carrington. McEnroe knuckled down enough to win the final set seven games to five. Even though the match had been a straight sets win, McEnroe had taken three hours to beat the Australian. The crowd jeered and booed as he left the court and the next day the *Daily Mirror* headlined their coverage, "Superbrat plays up for Lady Di" while the *Daily Express* went for "Beauty and the Beast".

Ticket touts were selling tickets for the final for £250 for a pair. The bookies gave odds of Borg to win at 4/6. The odds were slashed as the match began at 2pm to 1/3. McEnroe had written motivational notes for himself – throw the ball high, keep your head up, concentrate – and put them in his racquet case in case he needed to read them during the match. McEnroe served first and won the first game. The games went to serve until McEnroe double faulted and Borg took the lead 3-2. The psychological games began and Borg won the first set 6-4. In the second set, a wag called out "Why don't you call for the referee, John?" The crowd shushed and even Borg glanced over to the cat-caller. It unsettled McEnroe and he served a double fault. "Thank you very much," he called out to his tormentor, who did not repeat the jibe. When another close call occurred, the crowd expected McEnroe to again explode but he stared at the spot for 20 seconds before he walked to the receiver's end. A ripple of applause began on that side before echoing around the whole Centre Court. McEnroe maintained his composure to win the next three sets 7-6, 7-6, 6-4 and take the title. Borg said: "On all the important points, John hit his first serve. And that was crucial, especially in the tie-breakers."

ONLY

YEAR AT WIMBLEDON LADIES' SINGLES WINNER EARNED MORE THAN GENTLEMEN'S SINGLES WINNER

The Championships, Church Road, Wimbledon, London SW19 5AE England. Saturday, 4 July 1981

In 1981, the total prize money on offer at Wimbledon was £322,136 (£1,257,780 at 2020 values). The winner of the Gentlemen's Singles title (John McEnroe) earned £21,600 (£85,000, 2020) while the Ladies' Singles champion (Chris Evert) received £19,440 (£76,000, 2020). Chris Evert was also given a diamond necklace worth £3,000 (£11,750, 2020) which meant the prize for the Ladies' winner was greater than that for the Gentlemen's – the only time this has occurred in the history of The Championships.

FIRST

UNSEEDED MAN TO WIN THE FRENCH OPEN

Mats Wilander, Men's Singles, French Open, Stade Roland-Garros, 2 Avenue Gordon Bennett, 75016 Paris, France. Sunday, 6 June 1982

In 1980, Swede Mats Wilander made his debut as a tennis professional at the clay court tournament in Båstad, Sweden. The following year, he won the French Open Boys' title but was not expected to progress too far in the French Open and was thus unseeded. The four-time defending champion was Wilander's fellow Swede Björn Borg but he announced his retirement and John McEnroe, the world number one, pulled out of the French Open with an ankle injury. Number one seed was Jimmy Connors who was knocked out in the quarter-finals, with the rest of the top ten seeds comprising Ivan Lendl (fourth round), Guillermo Vilas (final), José Luis Clerc (semi-finalist), Vitas Gerulaitis (quarter-finalist), Eliot Teltscher (fourth round), Peter McNamara (quarter-finalist), Yannick Noah (quarter-finalist), Andrés Gómez (fourth round) and Balázs Taróczy (second round).

In the first round, Wilander saw off Colombian Alejandro Cortes 6-4, 6-3, 6-4. In the second, he beat Brazilian Cássio Motta 6-3, 6-4, 4-6, 6-2, then, in the third round, he came up against Fernando Luna Vicente and won with ease 6-3, 6-1, 6-0. He upset second seed Ivan Lendl in the fourth round 4-6, 7-5, 3-6, 6-4, 6-2 and beat fifth seed Vitas Gerulaitis in the quarter-final, 6-3, 6-3, 4-6, 6-4. In the semi-final, Wilander came up against fourth seed José Luis Clerc and won 7-5, 6-2, 1-6, 7-5. During that game, Wilander asked for a point that would have given him the match to be replayed because he thought the linesman's call was incorrect. The decision garnered Wilander praise from the sporting world and earned him the Pierre de Coubertin World Fair Play Trophy. In the final, he met third seed Guillermo Vilas and won 1-6, 7-6 (8-6), 6-0, 6-4 in four hours and 42 minutes. He became the youngest major tournament winner at 17 years and nine months – a record later surpassed by Boris Becker and Michael Chang. In 1983, Wilander lost in the French Open final to Yannick Noah (see 1983).

FIRST

FEMALE ATHLETE TO EARN MORE THAN $1,000,000 IN A YEAR

MARTINA NAVRATILOVA, 1982

Born in Prague, Czechoslovakia, on 18 October 1956 as Martina Šubertová, Navratilova asked the United States for political asylum in 1975. In 1981, she became an American citizen and the following year, she became the first female athlete (in any sport) to earn more than

$1,000,000 in a year. She retired from singles tennis in 1994 but in her career she was ranked world number one player in singles for 332 weeks and a record 237 weeks in doubles, making her **the only player in history to have held the top spot in both singles and doubles for more than 200 weeks**. She won 59 major titles comprising 18 Grand Slam singles titles, 31 major women's doubles titles (an all-time record), and ten major mixed doubles titles. Navratilova holds the records for most singles (167) and doubles titles (177) in the Open Era. She and Serena Williams are **the only Open Era players to have won six major singles crowns without the loss of a set**. On 9 January 2008, she once again became a Czech citizen.

LAST
FRENCHMAN TO WIN THE FRENCH OPEN

LAST
GRAND SLAM TITLE WON BY A PLAYER
WITH A WOODEN RACQUET

YANNICK NOAH, FRENCH OPEN, STADE ROLAND-GARROS, 2 AVENUE GORDON BENNETT, 75016 PARIS, FRANCE. SUNDAY, 5 JUNE 1983

Apart from the first year (see 1891) when it was won by a Briton, and an interruption for the First World War between 1915 and 1919, the French Open (then the Championnat de France) was won by a Frenchman every year from 1892 until 1932, when Australian Jack Crawford triumphed. A variety of nationalities were successful after the Second World War until the advent of the Open Era in 1968. The French competition was the first Grand Slam competition open to non-amateur players. Spaniard Rafael Nadal has won the most French Open titles – 12 (which is also a record for any player in the four major tournaments). Nadal also holds the record for the most consecutive wins in the Open Era, with five from 2010 until 2014.

Swede Mats Wilander won the French Open in 1982 but was only seeded number five in 1983, when Frenchman Yannick Noah was seeded one place below him. In the first round, Noah beat Swede Anders Per Järryd 6-1, 6-0, 6-2. In the second round, Noah beat Paraguayan Víctor Pecci, Sr 6-4, 6-3, 6-3. His opponent in the third round was American Patrick DuPré and Noah triumphed 7-5, 7-6, 6-2. Australian John Alexander was next up, but Noah won in straight sets, 6-2, 7-6, 6-1. In the quarter-final, he played Ivan Lendl, the Czech number three seed, and won 7-6, 6-2, 5-7, 6-0. In another quarter-final the unseeded Frenchman Christophe Roger-Vasselin had seen off the number one seed Jimmy Connors in straight sets. The seeding arrangement meant that there could not be an all-French final and, in the semis, Roger-Vasselin was no match for Noah who won in straight sets 6-3, 6-0, 6-0. Noah then beat Wilander in straight sets in the final, 6-2, 7-5, 7-6.

◆◆◆

FIRST

WOMAN UMPIRE OFFICIATING
A WIMBLEDON FINAL

GEORGINA CLARK, LADIES' SINGLES FINAL, THE CHAMPIONSHIPS, CHURCH ROAD, WIMBLEDON, LONDON SW19 5AE ENGLAND. SATURDAY, 7 JULY 1984

The first woman umpire did not appear on Centre Court until 1981 and it would be three more years before one would officiate at a final. Georgina Clark was born as Georgina Honor Lawrence in Hong Kong, where her father worked for BP, on 16 January 1940. She married John Clark when she was 18 and had five children within ten years. In 1981, she formally warned John McEnroe for his unsportsmanlike behaviour in the Queen's Club final. She was in the chair for the 1984 Wimbledon Ladies' Singles final between Martina Navratilova and Chris Evert. Navratilova beat Evert 7-6, 6-2 to retain her title and win for the sixth time. In 2005, Mrs Clark was afflicted by progressive supranuclear palsy, a degenerative neurological condition. She died aged 70 on 28 February 2010.

FIRST

UNSEEDED PLAYER TO WIN
WIMBLEDON GENTLEMEN'S SINGLES TITLE

FIRST

GERMAN TO WIN WIMBLEDON
GENTLEMEN'S SINGLES TITLE

Boris Becker, Gentlemen's Singles, The
Championships, Church Road, Wimbledon, London.
SW19 5AE England. Sunday, 7 July 1985

Boris Franz Becker was born on 22 November 1967 at Leimen, south of
Heidelberg, West Germany, the son of Karl-Heinz Becker, an architect.
He began playing tennis in earnest when he was six, in 1974, and joined
TC Blau-Weiß Leimen tennis club. In 1977, Becker became a member
of the Baden Tennis Association junior side and proceeded to win the
South German Championship and the first German Youth Tennis
Tournament. Recognising an emerging talent, the German Tennis
Federation paid for Becker's training at a cost of more than 1.3 million
Deutsche Marks. In 1984, Becker became a professional and won his
first professional doubles title that year in Munich. In 1985, he won the
Tennis World Young Masters at the NEC in Birmingham and then won
the singles title at Queen's Club in June, beating Johan Kriek 6-2, 6-3.

Three of Becker's first six games at Wimbledon were suspended.
In his opening game at The Championships, Becker beat American
Hank Pfister 4-6, 6-3, 6-2, 6-4. In the second round, he beat American
qualifier M. Anger 6-0, 6-1, 6-3. In the third round, he was up against
the Swede Joakim Nyström, who took him to five sets, but Becker won
3-6, 7-6, 6-1, 4-6, 9-7. The fourth round was another five-setter, with
Becker beating the American Tim Mayotte 6-3, 4-6, 6-7 (7-9), 7-6 (7-5),
6-2. In the fourth set, Becker injured his ankle and wanted to quit but

his Romanian manager Ion Ţiriac persuaded him to continue. In reality, Mayotte should have won and Becker been disqualified for the time it took the German to have treatment on his injury.

The 6ft 3in, 17-year-old's quarter-final opponent was the unseeded Frenchman Henri Leconte and Becker won 7-6, 3-6, 6-3, 6-4. After that match, the bookies Ladbrokes made Becker 7/4 favourite to win the competition. German television interrupted its normal schedule to broadcast the quarter-final live. The British press took every opportunity to remind their readers that Becker was German. Rex Bellamy wrote in *The Times* when he learned of the television change, "How odd it was that Germany should have such a personal interest on which, in 1940, they dropped a bomb." (The Luftwaffe dropped a bomb on Wimbledon on 11 October 1940 and destroyed 1,200 Centre Court seats. Wimbledon resumed in 1946 but all Germans were banned from the tournament for four years.)

In the semi-final, which began on the Friday and thanks to rain was finished on the day before the final, the young German met the number five seed Anders Järryd from Sweden. Järryd took the first set 6-2, but Becker fought back to win 7-6 (7-3), 6-3, 6-3. In the final, which lasted three hours and 18 minutes, Becker played the number eight seed Kevin Curren who had become an American citizen in March 1985. In the quarter-final, 27-year-old Curren had beaten defending champion John McEnroe and then went past Jimmy Connors in the semi-final, becoming the first player to beat Connors and McEnroe in the same Grand Slam tournament.

In front of 13,118 spectators, Becker won the first set in the final 6-3 in 35 minutes. Curren won the second 7-6 (7-4) but Becker won the next two sets 7-6 (7-3), 6-4 to take the title and become the youngest male Grand Slam singles champion at 17 years and 227 days (a record that would be broken in 1989 by Michael Chang, who was 17 years and 110 days old when he won the French Open). Becker had served 21 aces to Curren's 19 on the way to the trophy. Afterwards Curren said, "I should have had the advantage. Being older, being to the semi-finals before, being on Centre Court. Maybe he was too young to know about all that stuff. I couldn't imagine that I'd beat both McEnroe and Connors in the same tournament – and not win it. He never had to play a McEnroe or a Connors but what Becker did was a sign of great maturity for someone that young. He's got the qualities of a champion. At 17, I would have been totally intimidated by the whole atmosphere."

Becker said, "I'm the first German and I will think that will change tennis in Germany. They never had an idol before and now maybe they have one." In 1986, Becker successfully retained his Wimbledon title, defeating the number one player Ivan Lendl in straight sets in the final. In 1987, Becker was expected to do well but was knocked out in the second round by Peter Doohan, then rated number 70 in the world. In 1988, Becker reached the final but lost to Stefan Edberg in four sets.

TENNIS TALK

"The plan from my parents for me was to finish school, go to university, get a proper degree and learn something respectful. The last thing on everyone's mind was me becoming a tennis professional."

Boris Becker

ONLY

SINGLES TOURNAMENT WON BY ANNABEL CROFT

Women's Singles, Southern California Open, San Diego Hilton Beach & Tennis Resort, 1775 East Mission Bay Drive, San Diego, California 92109, United States of America. Sunday, 28 April 1985

In 1985, 18-year-old Annabel Croft won the Southern California Open played on outdoor hard courts at the San Diego Hilton Beach & Tennis Resort in San Diego. The thoughts of Britons everywhere turned to the possibility of a new tennis superstar, as unseeded Croft won the singles title beating the number seven seed Wendy Turnbull 6-0, 7-6 (7-5). It turned out to be yet another false dawn as it was the only title Croft ever won and she retired from the professional game in 1988 aged 21.

ONLY

PLAYER AT WIMBLEDON TO
WEAR AN ALL-IN-ONE BODYSUIT

ANNE WHITE, LADIES' SINGLES, THE CHAMPIONSHIPS, CHURCH ROAD, WIMBLEDON, LONDON SW19 5AE ENGLAND. THURSDAY, 27 JUNE 1985

Wimbledon has a rule that all players must wear outfits that are predominantly white. Anne White was drawn against fifth seed Pam Shriver in the first round at Wimbledon and warmed up wearing a tracksuit. When the match began, she took off the tracksuit to reveal an all-in-one white Lycra bodysuit. The game was balanced at one set all when bad light stopped play. Afterwards, Alan Mills, the tournament referee, suggested the next day she wear something more appropriate. She wore a regulation top and skirt and lost 6-3, 6-7, 6-3. She later said, "I was 24 years old. Would I do it now? Absolutely not. But I believed in it and hopefully, it looked nice. To me it made sense. I had no idea it would be so controversial." At the time, she said, "I'm a little aggravated I couldn't wear it today. But it's their tournament and I don't want to do something to upset them or hurt their feelings. I mean I don't want people spilling their strawberries and cream because of me."

DID YOU KNOW?

At the French Open in 2018, Serena Williams wore a black catsuit that was subsequently banned. French Open president Bernard Giudicelli said, "I believe we have gone too far. Serena's outfit this year will no longer be accepted. You have to respect the game and the place."

FIRST

WIMBLEDON CHAMPIONSHIPS
TO USE YELLOW BALLS

The Championships, Church Road, Wimbledon, London SW19 5AE
England. Monday, 23 June – Sunday, 6 July 1986

For the first time The Championships started using yellow balls so that television viewers would be able to see them more clearly.

ONLY

YEAR SINCE THE SECOND WORLD WAR
A MEMBER OF THE ROYAL FAMILY
HAS NOT PRESENTED THE TROPHY TO THE
WIMBLEDON SINGLES CHAMPIONS

THE CHAMPIONSHIPS, CHURCH ROAD, WIMBLEDON, LONDON SW19 5AE ENGLAND.
SATURDAY, 5 JULY – SUNDAY, 6 JULY 1986

In 1986, Wimbledon celebrated the 100th championships and in recognition of the milestone The Championships invited the two oldest living singles champions to present the Singles Championship trophies. Frenchman Jean Borotra – one of the Four Musketeers – who won the Gentlemen's Singles in 1924 and 1936 handed the trophy to Boris Becker – the youngest winner of the Gentlemen's Singles. Kitty Godfree, who won the Ladies' Singles in the same years that Borotra triumphed in the Gentlemen's, handed the Ladies' trophy to Martina Navratilova. Borotra died on 17 July 1994 at the age of 95. Godfree died on 19 June 1992 at the age of 96.

ONLY

GRAND SLAM WINNER TO MARRY
AN ACADEMY AWARD WINNER

JOHN MCENROE, ST DOMINIC'S CATHOLIC CHURCH, 93 ANSTICE
STREET, OYSTER BAY, NEW YORK 11771, UNITED STATES OF
AMERICA. FRIDAY, 1 AUGUST 1986

In October 1984, John McEnroe met Tatum O'Neal at a party held at the
Beverly Hills home of the record producer Richard Perry. He was with
Vitas Gerulaitis and she was with Victoria Sellers, the daughter of Britt
Ekland and Peter Sellers. O'Neal later said that McEnroe was shocked
that she did not go home with him. "I was never one for jumping into
strange men's beds," she said, "and, besides, I was pretty heavily into coke
at the time, which wasn't the greatest aphrodisiac." On 2 April 1974
O'Neal had won an Oscar for Best Supporting Actress for the film *Paper
Moon*, which was made when she was ten. Playing opposite her father,
Ryan O'Neal, the young actress had stolen every scene.

"He [McEnroe] was very good-looking. I thought he was charming
… It was sort of a chemical attraction or physical attraction, a love at first
sight kind of thing." In September 1985, O'Neal, who was four years
younger than McEnroe, discovered that she was pregnant. McEnroe
decided to take the first half of 1986 off to spend time with Tatum and
their new-born son Kevin Jack, who arrived on 23 May 1986. They
married that year and son Sean Timothy was born on 23 September
1987 with Emily Katherine following on 10 May 1991. The couple
had an acrimonious split in October 1992, McEnroe filed for divorce
on 8 January 1993 and they were divorced in 1994. Initially, they were
awarded joint custody of their children, with O'Neal awarded primary
care. However, in 1998 McEnroe was awarded sole custody. Both flung
accusations of drug abuse at the other. O'Neal became a heroin addict
after McEnroe married rock singer Patty Smyth and her mother died
in 1997. After court proceedings, O'Neal's visits with her children were
restricted, and she was required to submit to urine drug testing regularly,
in order to see them. O'Neal acknowledged that her heroin addiction
made her unfit to take care of her children. "I knew that he needed

to take care of the children. I knew that I needed help. That doesn't mean he needed to call me a scum-sucking pig," she said. In July 1999, their 13-year-old son Kevin had discovered his father's marijuana and smoked it. McEnroe said, "Not all my son's familial role models took a … strict line [on drugs]. I don't want to go into my ex-wife's side of the family, but let's just say if you were looking for a stabilising influence as a grandparent, you probably wouldn't choose Ryan O'Neal."

TENNIS TALK

"Nobody beats Vitas Gerulaitis 17 times in a row."

Vitas Gerulaitis on finally beating Jimmy Connors (in the Masters Championships at Madison Square Garden, having lost the previous 16 matches, 12 January 1980

FIRST
SENIOR FINAL FEATURING TWO BLACK WOMEN
LORI MCNEIL V ZINA GARRISON, ECKERD OPEN, BARDMOOR COUNTRY CLUB, 8001 CUMBERLAND ROAD, SEMINOLE, FLORIDA 33777, UNITED STATES OF AMERICA. SUNDAY, 21 SEPTEMBER 1986

In the 1980s, long before the Williams sisters dominated ladies' tennis, Lori McNeil and Zina Garrison were top players. McNeil, whose father, Charlie, was a defensive back for the San Diego Chargers, turned professional in 1983. When she met Garrison in the Eckerd Open final, McNeil beat her friend 2-6, 7-5, 6-2. In 1994, she knocked reigning champion Steffi Graf out of Wimbledon in the first round – 7-5, 7-6 (7-5).

The youngest of seven children, Garrison started playing tennis aged ten. In 1981, she won both the Wimbledon and US Open junior titles and was rated the world number one junior player. Aged 19, after the death of her mother, she began suffering from bulimia. "I had never been comfortable with my looks and felt I had lost the only person who loved me unconditionally," she said. "The pressure of being labelled 'the next Althea Gibson' only made things worse. I felt I was never going to be allowed to grow into just becoming me." Garrison turned professional in

1982, the year she was made the WTA Newcomer of the Year. In 1985, she reached the semi-final at Wimbledon. With Pam Shriver, she won the Women's Doubles gold medal at the 1988 Olympic Games in Seoul, beating Jana Novotná and Helena Suková of Czechoslovakia. In 1990, she beat Monica Seles and world number one Steffi Graf before losing to Martina Navratilova 6-4, 6-1 in the Ladies' Singles at Wimbledon. Garrison retired from professional tennis in 1996.

LAST
TIME A WOODEN RACQUET USED AT WIMBLEDON
THE CHAMPIONSHIPS, CHURCH ROAD, WIMBLEDON, LONDON SW19 5AE ENGLAND. 1987

The last time a wooden racquet was used at Wimbledon was in 1987. Today most racquets are made from carbon fibre reinforced with Kevlar, graphite and titanium.

DID YOU KNOW?

In 1986, Boris Becker's Romanian manager Ion Țiriac arranged for the Catholic German to have an audience with Pope John Paul II. Becker took his racquet with him to get it blessed by the Holy Father.

LAST
TIME CHRIS EVERT APPEARED IN A MAJOR FINAL
Women's Singles v Steffi Graf, Australian Open, Flinders Park, Batman Avenue, Melbourne 3000 Australia. Saturday, 23 January 1988

Born on 21 December 1954 at Fort Lauderdale, Florida, Chris Evert began playing tennis when she was five. Evert made her Grand Slam tournament debut at age 16 at the US Open in September 1971.

Unseeded, she lost in the semi-final to Billie Jean King. Two years later, she was the runner-up at the French Open (defeated by number one seed Margaret Court 6-7, 7-6, 6-4) and the Wimbledon Championships (losing to King 6-0, 7-5). In 1974, she won both titles, beating Olga Morozova in both finals 6-1, 6-2 and 6-0, 6-4 respectively. With her then boyfriend Jimmy Connors, she finished runner-up at the 1974 US Open in Mixed Doubles. In 1975 she won her second French Open (defeating Martina Navratilova 2-6, 6-2, 6-1) and the first of four straight US Open championships. In 1976, she won Wimbledon and the US Open – the only time she won both titles in the same year. In 1979 and 1980, she won the French Open, beating Wendy Turnbull and Virginia Ruzici in the finals. Her last Grand Slam title came at the 1986 French Open, where she beat Martina Navratilova in three sets. On 21 January 1988, aged 33, she beat Navratilova in straight sets in the semi-final of the Australian Open to reach her 34th and last Grand Slam final. In her 34 finals, Evert won 18 Grand Slam singles titles: seven at the French Open (a record for a female player), six at the US Open (an Open Era record, male or female, tied with Serena Williams), three at Wimbledon, and two at the Australian Open (both on grass). Additionally, Evert won three Grand Slam doubles titles, at the French in 1974 with Olga Morozova, in 1975 with Navratilova, and again with Navratilova at Wimbledon in 1976. Evert retired from the professional tour after the US Open in 1989.

ONLY
PLAYER TO WIN A GOLDEN SLAM

Steffi Graf, v Chris Evert, Women's Singles, Australian Open, Flinders Park, Batman Avenue, Melbourne 3000 Australia. Saturday, 23 January 1988; v Natalia Zvereva, Women's Singles, French Open Stade Roland-Garros, 2 Avenue Gordon Bennett, 75016 Paris, France. 1988; v Martina Navratilova, Ladies' Singles, The Championship, Church Road, Wimbledon, London. SW19 5AE England. Saturday, 2 July 1988; v Gabriela Sabatini, Women's Singles, US Open, USTA National Tennis Center, Flushing Meadows-Corona Park, Flushing, New York 11368, United States of America. Saturday, 10 September 1988; v Gabriela Sabatini, Women's Singles, Olympic Games, Seoul, South Korea. Saturday, 1 October 1988

In January 1988 Steffi Graf won the first of her three consecutive Australian Open titles. Seeded number one, she beat Chris Evert 6-1, 7-6 (7-3), having defeated reigning champion Hana Mandlíková in the quarter-final. With Graf leading 2-1 in the first set, it began to rain and the match was delayed for one hour and 23 minutes to close the retractable roof, making this **the first Grand Slam final played under a roof**. Graf won 6-1, 7-6 (7-3) with Evert admitting, "Steffi is a much better indoor player than I am." In France she successfully defended her title by beating Natalia Zvereva in the final, 6-0, 6-0 – the only double bagel Grand Slam final of the Open Era. The match lasted just 32 minutes. Graf didn't drop a set in the entire tournament. At Wimbledon she met Martina Navratilova in the final and won 5-7, 6-2, 6-1 to capture her first Ladies' Singles title and the next segment of the Grand (Golden) Slam. Gabriela Sabatini proved no match for Graf at the US Open, losing 6-3, 3-6, 6-1 as the German took the Grand Slam. Said Graf after the match, "I'm very happy all the talk of the Grand Slam is over. That's a nice relief. Now I've done it and there's no more pressure on me. There's nothing else you can tell me that I have to do." Three weeks later, she was playing Gabriela Sabatini in the Olympic Games in Seoul and won 6-3, 6-3 to take the gold medal and the Golden Slam. "I'm very excited," said Graf, "it's amazing."

LAST

WIGHTMAN CUP

UNITED STATES V UNITED KINGDOM, THE COLLEGE OF WILLIAM & MARY, WILLIAMSBURG, VIRGINIA 23185 UNITED STATES OF AMERICA. SEPTEMBER 1989

The United States won the inaugural Wightman Cup in 1923 by seven games to love and then the following year the United Kingdom exacted revenge by winning 6-1. The United Kingdom won the 1925 cup by the closer margin of 4-3. But then the United States began to assert itself and, pre-war, the United Kingdom won the cup just four times. Post-war, they did not triumph until 1958. Until 1960 all editions of the Wightman Cup were played on grass; in later years they also used clay courts, cement and synthetic carpet. In 1967, the 39th cup was held at the Cleveland Arena in Ohio and for the first time took place over three days rather than two, to raise revenue. It worked, as a record 16,000 spectators attended.

In 1974, **the Wightman Cup was held outside England and America for the only time** when it was staged at the Deeside Leisure Centre, Queensferry, Wales. The United Kingdom won 6-1. The 1978 cup was moved indoors to the Royal Albert Hall and was sponsored for the first time. The United Kingdom won 4-3 and it was **the last victory for the UK**. The last 11 cups were all won by the United States. The 61st and final Wightman Cup was held in Williamsburg, Virginia, and was a 7-0 whitewash for the States. In the opening match, Lori McNeil won five of the last six games in the first set and the last five games of the second set to defeat Jo Durie 7-5, 6-1. On 14 September 1989, the second match was between 13-year-old Jennifer Capriati and Clare Wood, which the teenager won 6-0, 6-0. Capriati was the youngest player to play in the Wightman Cup, besting the previous record by two years. By 1989, the competition was looking completely one-sided with the United States winning the trophy 51 times to the United Kingdom's ten. On 20 February 1990, the United States Tennis Association and the Lawn Tennis Association announced that the Wightman Cup would be suspended indefinitely.

<hr>

FIRST
AUSTRALIAN OPEN MEN'S FINAL TO END IN RETIREMENT

MEN'S SINGLES, AUSTRALIAN OPEN, FLINDERS PARK, BATMAN AVENUE, MELBOURNE 3000 AUSTRALIA. SUNDAY, 28 JANUARY 1990

Reigning champion and number one seed Ivan Lendl retained his Australian Open crown when his opponent Stefan Edberg retired because of a torn stomach muscle. Lendl was leading 4-6, 7-6 (7-3), 5-2 when the Swede announced that he could not continue. It was the first time in 85 years of the competition that a men's finalist could not finish the match (see 2006). Edberg had hurt himself in the semi-final win over fellow Swede Mats Wilander two days earlier.

LAST
YEAR SPECTATORS COULD STAND ON CENTRE COURT, WIMBLEDON

The Championships, Centre Court, Wimbledon, Church Road, Wimbledon, London SW19 5AE England. Sunday, 8 July 1990

In much the same way all grounds at Premier League and The Championships are all-seating, Wimbledon followed suit after the tournament in 1990. Until that year, there was room for 2,000 spectators to stand and cheer. Now, it is all seating.

FIRST
ALL-GERMAN WIMBLEDON GENTLEMEN'S SINGLES FINAL
LAST
WIMBLEDON COMMENTARY BY DAN MASKELL

MICHAEL STICH V BORIS BECKER, GENTLEMEN'S SINGLES FINAL, THE CHAMPIONSHIPS, CHURCH ROAD, WIMBLEDON, LONDON SW19 5AE ENGLAND. SUNDAY, 7 JULY 1991

Born at 15 Everington Street, Fulham, southwest London on 11 April 1908, the seventh of eight children, Dan Maskell began his tennis career in 1923 when he became a ball boy at Queen's Club for ten shillings a week. Maskell first went to Wimbledon in 1924 to watch the Ladies'

Singles final (Kitty McKane – later Godfree – beat Helen Wills: the only match Wills lost in nine visits to the tournament) and said he never missed a day's play from 1929 until 1991. By 1926 he had a five-year contract to teach lawn tennis, real tennis, rackets and squash at Queen's. In October 1927, Maskell arranged the first World Professional Championships – a competition he won beating Charles Read. The following year, Maskell became British professional champion, a title he would hold 15 more times, until 1951. In 1929, he joined the All England Lawn Tennis and Croquet Club at Wimbledon as their first professional coach, a position he held until 1955. He was coach of the winning British Davis Cup team of 1933.

During the Second World War, he joined the Royal Air Force and worked rehabilitating injured air crew at the Palace Hotel, Torquay, and then Loughborough. He was demobbed with the rank of squadron leader and an OBE. In 1949, he joined BBC Radio as an analyst and in 1951 moved to television, where he became synonymous with the BBC coverage of tennis. Maskell's catchphrase when describing a good shot or play was "Oh, I say!" In 1953, he became the first professional to be admitted as an honorary member of the All England Club. He retired as a player in 1955 and joined the Lawn Tennis Association as its training manager, a job he held until 1973. He was appointed CBE in 1982 for services to tennis. He became close to the Royal Family and coached Princess Alexandra, the Prince of Wales, the Princess Royal (he believed she could have been a great player had she had time to work at the game) and the Duke of York.

The last Wimbledon match that Maskell commentated on was the 1991 Gentlemen's Singles final between Michael Stich and Boris Becker. The last tennis match he commentated on for BBC Television was the 1991 Grand Slam Cup final between David Wheaton and Michael Chang. He died in his sleep of heart failure on 10 December 1992, at East Surrey Hospital in Redhill. He played with all the great players and rated as his best Rod Laver among the men and Martina Navratilova among the women.

ONLY
WIMBLEDON CHAMPION TO DIE OF AIDS
ARTHUR ASHE, NEW YORK HOSPITAL, PRAVEEN HOSPITAL LANE, NEW YORK 10032 UNITED STATES OF AMERICA. SATURDAY, 6 FEBRUARY 1993

In New York in July 1979, while teaching tennis, Arthur Ashe had a heart attack. He was 36. Although a superbly fit athlete, heart disease ran in Ashe's family. His mother, Mattie Cordell Cunningham Ashe, had died when she was 27 from pre-eclampsia having suffered from cardiovascular disease. His father had two heart attacks, the second just a week before his son's. Having discovered that one of his arteries was totally shut, another was 95 per cent closed and a third was half closed in two places, Ashe underwent a quadruple bypass operation on 13 December 1979. In 1983, Ashe underwent a second round of surgery. Five years later, in September 1988, Ashe found his right arm was paralysed. Tests showed that he was infected with toxoplasmosis, a disease commonly associated with people suffering from HIV. Ashe underwent more tests and it was discovered he was HIV positive and had probably contracted the disease during his second heart surgery. Ashe and his wife kept the news quiet for the sake of their daughter, but on 8 April 1992, Ashe pre-empted *USA Today*, who were going to run a story exposing his condition, by making the admission himself. Ashe died aged 49 from Aids-related pneumonia less than a year later. His funeral was held at the Arthur Ashe Athletic Center in Richmond, Virginia, on 10 February.

ONLY
GRAND SLAM WINNER
STABBED ON COURT
Monica Seles, Citizen Cup, Am Rothenbaum Tennis Club, Hallerstraße 89, 20149 Hamburg, Germany. Friday, 30 April 1993

Born in Yugoslavia on 2 December 1973, Monica Seles began playing tennis when she was five. She won the French Open three years on the trot – 1990, 1991 and 1992 – and the Australian Open in 1991, 1992 and 1993. She won the US Open in 1991 and 1992 and was a Wimbledon finalist into 1992. Her career appeared on the up and up and she was the top-ranked female player in the world. On 31 January 1993, she beat number two seed Steffi Graf 4-6, 6-3, 6-2 to win the Australian Open – her third consecutive victory in the competition and her third win in four Grand Slam finals against Graf.

Three months later, Seles was playing in the Citizen Cup at Hamburg, Germany. She made it to the quarter-finals, where she was drawn against Magdalena Maleeva – the youngest national tennis champion of Bulgaria. Seles was leading and on a serve break when a man ran from the crowd and plunged a boning knife between Seles's shoulder blades to a depth of 0.59 inches. Seles was taken to hospital where the injury was found not to be serious. The man was taken into custody and discovered to be Günter Parche, an obsessed fan of Steffi Graf. At his trial, Parche was found to be mentally abnormal and sentenced to two years' probation and psychological treatment. Seles was not impressed by the result. "What people seem to be forgetting is that this man stabbed me intentionally and he did not serve any sort of punishment for it … I would not feel comfortable going back [to play in Germany]. I don't foresee that happening." It would be almost three years before Seles won another major competition. On 27 January 1996, she beat Anke Huber 6-4, 6-1 to win the Australian Open. She said, "Standing up and holding that trophy I held in '93, I thought I was going to hold in '94, not being able to do that in '95 and now in '96, again holding it, it's very special."

ONLY

GRAND SLAM FINALIST TO CRY

ON A ROYAL SHOULDER

JANA NOVOTNÁ, LADIES' SINGLES FINAL, THE

CHAMPIONSHIP, CHURCH ROAD, WIMBLEDON, LONDON
SW19 5AE ENGLAND. SATURDAY, 3 JULY 1993

Steffi Graf won Wimbledon in 1992 and was the number one seed for the 1993 Championships. Martina Navratilova was number two and down the list Jana Novotná was at number eight. Born in Brno, Czechoslovakia on 2 October 1968, Novotná turned professional in February 1987, the year after she first played at Wimbledon. In 1990, she reached the quarter-final, her best result until 1993. That year, Novotná made her way to the quarter-final where she faced Argentine number four seed Gabriela Sabatini. Novotná had lost six consecutive matches against the Argentine at that point, but this time the South American was no competition and lost in straight sets 6-4, 6-3. In the semi-final, Novotná beat Navratilova 6-4, 6-4 to face Graf in the final. The first set was tight and Graf won on a tie-break. Novotná took the second set 6-1 and then had a game-point serving at 4-1 in the third set, but then lost her nerve and lost 6-4. The Duchess of Kent appeared on Centre Court to present the winner's plate. It all became too much for Novotná and she burst into tears. The Duchess put her arm around the distraught player who sobbed on her shoulder. Novotná would appear in two more Ladies' finals, eventually winning the title in 1998.

She retired the next year and in 2000 began working as a commentator for the BBC. In 2010, she returned to her native Czech Republic, where she lived with her lover Iwona Kuczyńska, a former player. She died of cancer on 19 November 2017, aged 49. She was inducted into the International Tennis Hall of Fame in 2005.

FIRST
TIME TENNIS PLAYED INDOORS ON GRASS
HALLE OPEN, GERRY WEBER STADION, ROGER-FEDERER-ALLEE 4, 33790
HALLE (WESTFALEN), GERMANY. THURSDAY, 16 JUNE 1994

The Halle Open began in 1993 and the first singles was won by Henri Leconte while the doubles saw Petr Korda and Cyril Suk triumph. A whole day was lost to rain on 16 June 1993, which gave the organisers the idea of a roof to enable play to continue. Construction began on 19 July 1993 and the work took three months. The centre court has a roof made of PVC-coated polyester fabric and foil, that can be closed in 88 seconds if bad weather threatens play. The roof was first used on 16 June 1994.

FIRST

PLAYERS DISQUALIFIED FOR
HITTING A BALL GIRL

Tim Henman and Jeremy Bates, Gentlemen's Doubles, the
Championships, Church Road, Wimbledon, London SW19 5AE
England. Wednesday, 28 June 1995

In the first round of the Wimbledon Championships in 1995, Tim Henman won his first match in a Grand Slam event, beating Kenyan Paul Wekesa in straight sets, 7-6, 6-0, 6-4. In the second round, however, he was drawn against defending champion Pete Sampras and was knocked out 6-2, 6-3, 7-6. In the Doubles, Henman and Jeremy Bates were drawn on Court 14 against American Jeff Tarango and Swede Henrik Holm. Henman and Bates won the first set 7-6, lost the second 6-2, won the third 6-3 and the fourth set was on a tie-break at 6-6. Henman, frustrated that he had lost a point to a net cord, served but had not noticed that 16-year-old ball girl Caroline Hall was scampering across the net to collect a stray ball. She took the full force of Henman's serve on her left ear and collapsed to the ground, but only for a second, before, showing true British pluck, she got up and finished her job. After a brief chat with tournament referee Alan Mills, Australian umpire Wayne McKewen disqualified Henman and Bates for unsportsmanlike conduct. The Britons were ruled to have committed a code violation and were thrown out of the tournament. On the verge of tears at a late-night press conference at the All England Club, Henman said, "I was not happy at losing the point and was angry. I went to hit the ball hard. I'd looked to see if the lines-people were out of the way. It's a complete accident, but I'm responsible for my actions." A spokesman for Mr Mills said, "In the tie-break of the fourth set there was a net cord at a crucial point. In sheer frustration at missing it, Tim Henman slammed the ball which unfortunately hit a ball girl extremely hard on the side of the head. The rules precisely state that a player must be in control of his actions on court, and in such cases there is no choice but to default automatically on the basis of unsportsmanlike conduct. The ball girl, Caroline Hall, has been taken home and will undergo a thorough medical examination. Tim Henman is extremely upset about this freak accident, and although rare, the rules clearly state that default is the only course of action in cases of this nature."

Caroline recalled, "I think I'd been on court about ten minutes when Henman lost a point during a tie-break, hit a ball in anger and I got in the way. You're trained to just carry on no matter what, so that's what I did. I didn't feel that bad and besides, I was 16 and I didn't want to lose face. I didn't think any more of it until Bates came over, then all of a sudden the tournament referee, Alan Mills, was on court and it was chaos. I was sat down and got an ice pack on my face. Apparently, the ball was clocked at 92mph, and it did hurt a bit, but I'd have carried on if I could. No one asked my opinion but I was saying 'No, no, don't disqualify him.' Nothing was meant by it at all, it was just bad timing that meant the ball hit my head instead of going into the net. Alan Mills was really quite angry with him, which didn't seem very fair. After a few minutes, the umpire announced that the match was over. The crowd was booing; it was really terrible. It was a complete accident. I was unlucky, as was Tim. He has said sorry but I've already forgiven him. I know he didn't mean to hit me." In addition, Henman was fined £1,910 (£3,750 at 2020 values).

DID YOU KNOW?

Ironically, a few days later, Jeff Tarango was disqualified during a third-round match against Alexander Mronz of Germany after he questioned the impartiality of umpire Bruno Rebeuh. After the match, Benedicte Tarango slapped Herr Rebeuh "to teach him a lesson". Oddly, Caroline Hall was one of the ball girls at that match too.

ONLY
TIME SIR CLIFF RICHARD SANG AT WIMBLEDON

RICHARD KRAJICEK V PETE SAMPRAS, GENTLEMEN'S SINGLES QUARTER-FINAL, THE CHAMPIONSHIPS, CHURCH ROAD, WIMBLEDON, LONDON SW19 5AE ENGLAND. WEDNESDAY, 3 JULY 1996

The one thing that no one should take for granted in Britain is the weather. Rain is likely even at the height of summer. This was the case at the Gentlemen's Singles quarter-final match between Richard Krajicek v Pete Sampras. Play began at 12.30pm and the score was two games each when it began to rain and rain and rain. Three hours later, it was still raining. In the ground that day was the pop singer Sir Cliff Richard. Would he mind entertaining the bedraggled crowds? He wouldn't mind at all.

In the Royal Box, he was handed a microphone and began, naturally enough, with "Summer Holiday". Pam Shriver was getting a massage downstairs and saw Sir Cliff on the television singing. She said to Martina Navratilova: "This is our world, and he's helping us out. Let's go and help him." As Sir Cliff continued with "Bachelor Boy" and "Livin' Doll", he was joined by a backing group of Shriver, Navratilova, Gigi Fernandez, and Virginia Wade. Cliff performed six songs over 20 minutes to an audience that included Prince and Princess Michael of Kent and Joanna Lumley. And as he launched into "Congratulations", with the crowd clapping away, the sun came out, the covers were rolled back and play was restored.

TENNIS TALK

"He can't cook."

Michael Chang on Pete Sampras's weaknesses

ONLY

STREAKER AT GENTLEMEN'S
SINGLES FINAL AT WIMBLEDON

Melissa Johnson, Gentlemen's Singles final, The Championships, Church Road, Wimbledon, London SW19 5AE England. Sunday, 7 July 1996

Before the Gentlemen's Singles final, the bookmakers William Hill offered odds of 4/1 for a streaker to interrupt the match between Richard Krajicek and MaliVai Washington. It was too much for someone to resist and 23-year-old blonde London student Melissa Johnson was that someone. Prior to the warm-up and wearing just a maid's apron, she vaulted the barrier and ran the length of the court lifting her apron to give both players an eyeful before doing the same to the Royal Box, before she was led away. The Duke and Duchess of Kent and Prince and Princess Michael of Kent were visibly amused. Washington walked back to the baseline to begin his warm-up, lifted his shirt to reveal his bare chest and received a huge ovation from the 14,000-strong crowd. A Wimbledon spokesman said, "Whilst we do not wish to condone the practice, it did at least provide some light amusement for our loyal and patient supporters, who have had a trying time during the recent bad weather." Melissa Johnson was taken to Wimbledon police station and kept there for the duration of the final before she was released without further action. It took Krajicek 94 minutes to beat the unseeded American 6-3, 6-4, 6-3 and become **the first Dutchman to win Wimbledon**. Washington recalled, "I look over and see this streaker. She lifted up the apron and she was smiling at me. I got flustered and three sets later I was gone; that was pretty funny."

FIRST

PROFESSIONAL MATCH FOR THE
WILLIAMS SISTERS

VENUS WILLIAMS V SERENA WILLIAMS, AUSTRALIAN OPEN,

In their first professional meeting 17-year-old Venus beats 16-year-old Serena 7-6 (7-4), 6-1 in the second round of the Australian Open. Venus said, "I kept seeing Serena across the net. It was a little bit odd, but it is to be expected. In the future, it will be the same … I feel good that I won. Even though it was Serena, I'm still a competitor." In the next round Venus beat Amélie Mauresmo and in the fourth she defeated Patty Schnyder. In the quarter-final, she lost to number two seed Lindsay Davenport.

TENNIS TALK

"I can't believe he is dumping me, his buddy for seven years, for a kid he's never seen before."

Paul Haarhuis on doubles partner Jacco Eltingh
leaving the US Open for the birth of his son, 1998

LAST
WIMBLEDON MATCH FOR BORIS BECKER
ONLY
WIMBLEDON CHAMPION TO
FATHER A CHILD ON A RESTAURANT STAIRCASE

BORIS BECKER, GENTLEMEN'S SINGLES, THE CHAMPIONSHIPS, CENTRE COURT, CHURCH ROAD, WIMBLEDON, LONDON SW19 5AE ENGLAND; NOBU, 19 OLD PARK LANE, MAYFAIR, LONDON W1K 1LB ENGLAND. THURSDAY, 1 JULY 1999

At Wimbledon in 1999 the unseeded former champion Boris Becker was despatched in the fourth round by number two seed Pat Rafter 6-3, 6-2, 6-3. Becker said later he had "cried my eyes out" that his career was over and wanted to go out for a few drinks. Becker's wife, Barbara, seven months pregnant with their second son, wanted him to stay at their hotel.

"She couldn't and wouldn't understand that she suddenly wasn't first in my priorities," said Becker. "I said, 'Just once more with the lads, Barbara, just once more to say farewell and then it's only you.' That didn't work. We rowed for two whole hours. Suddenly she was in pain and decided to check into hospital." Becker told his wife to call him if the baby was really on the way, then went out for the night.

By 11pm he was at the bar of the trendy Nobu restaurant in London. The kitchen was closed so Becker made do with lemon sorbet in vodka. Becker had been in Nobu a fortnight earlier and spotted waitress Angela Ermakova. That night, she was there again. "She looked directly at me, the look of the hunter that said, 'I want you'. There she was again, walking twice past the bar. And again, this look. A little while later she left her table for the loos. I followed her. Five minutes of small talk and then straight away into the nearest possible suitable corner and down to business. Afterwards she went off, I had another beer, paid and went back to my hotel. As there wasn't any news from the hospital, I went to bed around 2am. In the morning I went to Barbara: the pains were a false alarm. We packed our 28 tennis bags and suitcases and left England. As to the consequences of the previous evening I didn't have a second thought."

In February 2000, a fax arrived at his Munich office: "Dear Herr Becker, We met a little while ago in Nobu in London. The result of that meeting is now eight months old." Becker refused to detail "what we did or, rather, what we didn't do. But dammit this was impossible. This was absolutely impossible." Becker hired private detectives to follow the waitress, but changed his mind and decided to accept paternity, long before a secret DNA test in February 2001 confirmed that he was indeed the father of baby Anna, born on 22 March 2000 at the Chelsea and Westminster Hospital.

Becker and his wife split up in November 2000. Becker filed for divorce on 15 December 2000, two days before his seventh wedding anniversary. Becker was granted a divorce on 15 January 2001: his ex-wife Barbara received a $14.4 million settlement, their condominium on Fisher Island, Florida, and custody of their two sons. Becker said that he did not understand why women went for him. "I'm not especially rich, I'm not especially pretty, I'm no Adonis and my manhood isn't over-enormous. Sex is totally overvalued in our society … I was totally monogamous during my seven-year marriage. But I also think we men are not created to be monogamous for our whole lives." Ermakova had launched a £3.3 million paternity suit against Becker. The retired tennis player had described the incident as "the most expensive five seconds of my life".

TENNIS TALK

"The trouble with me is that every match I play against five opponents: umpire, crowd, ball boys, court, and myself."

Goran Ivanišević, 2000

FIRST
TENNIS PLAYER EMAIL VIRUS
ANNA KOURNIKOVA VIRUS, UNITED STATES OF AMERICA. FEBRUARY 2001

Anna Kournikova was born in Moscow in the Soviet Union on 7 June 1981. Blonde and beautiful, she is probably better known for her looks than her tennis ability. She never won a singles title although with Martina Hingis, she won doubles titles in Australia in 1999 and 2002. The two called themselves the Spice Girls of Tennis. Kournikova retired aged 21, due to serious back and spinal problems. She has three children by the pop star Enrique Iglesias. He has said of her, "You go through your good times, you go through your bad times. It's a tough thing for me to believe there's such a thing as the perfect relationship. I don't think that exists. Firstly, she's the coolest girl in the world. And she understands who I am, to the point where she's willing to sacrifice her personal time with me and let me do my music. It's a huge sacrifice and I respect that tremendously." At the height of her fame, her name was one of the most Googled. In February 2001, an email virus began circulating in the United States. It promised recipients a picture of Kournikova but when it was opened a virus infected computers. It did not delete any documents but it clogged up the email programme.

TENNIS TALK

"Thanks, but no. I want to be a winner."

Maria Sharapova on being
compared to Anna Kournikova

ONLY

WILD CARD TO WIN A
SINGLES TITLE AT WIMBLEDON

Goran Ivanišević, Gentlemen's Singles, The Championships, Church Road, Wimbledon, London SW19 5AE England. Sunday, 9 July 2001

In 1977, wild cards were introduced to the Wimbledon Championships. Wild cards are players whose world ranking does not guarantee them a place in the tournament but their public profile or previous performance would enhance the tournament. In 2001, Goran Ivanišević was given a wild card. A three-time losing finalist (in 1992 to Andre Agassi, then 1994 and 1998 to Pete Sampras), he was ranked number 125 in the world because of a shoulder injury. He knocked out Andy Roddick in the third round before disposing of Greg Rusedski in straight sets in the fourth. In the quarter-final, Ivanišević overcame Marat Safin, the number four seed, in four sets. He dented Henmania in the semi-final beating the Briton 7-5, 6-7 (6-8), 0-6, 7-6 (7-5), 6-3. In the final, he came up against Australian Pat Rafter who had seen off Agassi and Thomas Enqvist on his way to Centre Court. Ivanišević beat Rafter 6-3, 3-6, 6-3, 2-6, 9-7 to take the Gentlemen's Singles title. He was the first unseeded player to win it since Boris Becker in 1985.

FIRST

BLACK PLAYER RANKED
NO 1 PLAYER IN OPEN ERA

VENUS WILLIAMS, WOMEN'S TENNIS ASSOCIATION. MONDAY, 25 FEBRUARY 2002

Venus Williams was the first black player – man or woman – to be ranked number one in the world. She was named the second of all time (after Althea Gibson who was an amateur) by the Women's Tennis Association (WTA). Williams became the eleventh player so ranked and stayed on top for three weeks. On 8 July 2002, sister Serena took over the number one slot. The WTA began producing computerised rankings on 3 November 1975. The first number one was Chris Evert.

TENNIS TALK

"I don't think anyone ever feared him in the locker room."

Todd Martin on whether Pete Sampras had lost the fear factor in the changing room

LAST
YEAR AT WIMBLEDON PLAYERS HAD
TO BOW OR CURTSEY TO THE ROYAL BOX

THE CHAMPIONSHIPS, CHURCH ROAD, WIMBLEDON, LONDON SW19 5AE
ENGLAND. MONDAY, 23 JUNE – SUNDAY, 6 JULY 2003

Until 2003, as players left or entered Centre Court they would bow or curtsey to members of the Royal Family occupying the Royal Box. On 29 April 2003, the president of the All England Club, His Royal Highness the Duke of Kent, decided to abandon the tradition. Players are now only obliged to show deference if Her Majesty the Queen or HRH the Prince of Wales are attending The Championships.

FIRST
MAJOR TITLE WIN BY
AMÉLIE MAURESMO
FIRST
MAJOR WOMEN'S OPEN ERA TITLE
TO END IN RETIREMENT

WOMEN'S SINGLES, AUSTRALIAN OPEN, MELBOURNE PARK, BATMAN
AVENUE, MELBOURNE 3000 AUSTRALIA. SATURDAY, 28 JANUARY 2006

French player Amélie Mauresmo, the third seed, won her first major singles title in Australia in 2006, although in bizarre circumstances. Having won the first set 6-1, she was leading 2-0 in the second when Justine Henin-Hardenne said she could not continue because of stomach pains (see 1990). It was the third time in the tournament that an opponent had retired early. At the after-match press conference, Mauresmo said, "What can I say? Am I going to make controversy about that? No. That's not the day for this for me." The two women would face each other in the Wimbledon final and Mauresmo would win in three sets.

FIRST

USE OF HAWK-EYE

NASDAQ-100 OPEN, KEY BISCAYNE, FLORIDA, UNITED STATES OF AMERICA. WEDNESDAY, 22 MARCH 2006

A year before it arrived at Wimbledon (see 2007), Hawk-Eye was used in Florida. Jamea Jackson was the first player to challenge a call in her first-round match with Ashley Harkleroad. Using one of her two challenges, she questioned whether the opening point of the second set was indeed out. A review showed that the call was correct and the ball was indeed out. Jackson, who went on to win 7-5, 6-7, 7-5 said, "I just wanted to be the first."

FIRST

USE OF HAWK-EYE AT WIMBLEDON

Gentlemen's Singles, The Championships, Church Road, Wimbledon, London SW19 5AE England. Monday, 25 June 2007

In 2007, Hawk-Eye replaced Cyclops (see 1980) at the Wimbledon Championships to adjudge close calls. The first time it was used there was in the first-round match between Georgian Teymuraz Gabashvili and Roger Federer on Centre Court. In the opening game of the third set, after a rain delay of almost three hours, and serving at 30-15, Gabashvili challenged a line call which had ruled a Federer passing shot was in. The Georgian had the class and good grace to congratulate the female line judge for a correct decision when Hawk-Eye confirmed the ball had clipped the line.

LAST

YEAR WIMBLEDON SCOREBOARDS
USED THE HONORIFIC
FOR FEMALE PLAYERS

The Championships, Church Road, Wimbledon, London SW19 5AE
England. Monday, 23 June 2008 – Sunday, 6 July 2008

From the first time they set foot on court, lady players were awarded the honorific on the scoreboards (not so the gentleman). The umpires also used the same style. Billie Jean King was listed on the scoreboard as Mrs L.W. King and Chris Evert, during her marriage to John Lloyd, as Mrs J.M. Lloyd while Evonne Goolagong was Mrs R. Cawley. At Wimbledon, that came to an end with the 2008 tournament. From the 2009 Championships, all that etiquette went out of the window and spectators in the ground and on television never knew if the players were married or not. In 2019, the tournament dropped the honorific for women players completely. Alexandra Willis, the head of communications, content and digital for the All England Club, said: "We have got to move with the times. Hopefully, we surprise people with the way we do that. Some of the traditions – white clothing, playing on grass – are our greatest strengths. Others absolutely have to move with the times. You have to respect the wishes of the players. I suppose the challenge for us is how much you rewrite history."

A spokesman for the International Tennis Federation said: "There is nothing specific in the Grand Slam rulebook about how to address female players – it is a decision for each individual Grand Slam. As far as I am aware, only Wimbledon previously prefixed a female player's surname and they are now in line with the other Slams." Novak Djokovic said: "I thought that tradition was very unique and very special. I thought it was nice. It's definitely not easy to alter or change any traditions here that have been present for many years. It's quite surprising that they've done that."

LADIES' NAMES

A number of women players have used both maiden and married names during competitions. Here is a brief guide to some of those ladies.

Married name	Maiden name
Janet Adkisson	Janet Hopps
Shirley Brasher	Shirley Bloomer
Evonne Cawley	Evonne Goolagong
Chris Evert Lloyd	Chris Evert
Christine Janes	Christine Truman
Ann Jones	Ann Haydon
Billie Jean King	Billie Jean Moffitt

FIRST MATCH PLAYED ENTIRELY "INDOORS" AT WIMBLEDON

Andy Murray v Stanislas Wawrinka, The Championships, Church Road, Wimbledon, London SW19 5AE England. Monday, 29 June 2009

The one thing that players, spectators and tourists alike complain about in England is the weather. The rain hampers many an outdoor event, not just sporting ones. At Wimbledon, it became apparent that something had to be done, so a retractable roof was built in time for the 2009 Championships. The roof was tested at A Centre Court Celebration on Sunday, 17 May 2009, which featured exhibition matches involving Andre Agassi, Steffi Graf, Kim Clijsters and Tim Henman. The first championship match to take place under the roof was the completion of the fourth round Ladies' Singles match between Dinara Safina and Amélie Mauresmo. The first match to be played in its entirety under the roof was between Andy Murray and Stanislas Wawrinka on 29 June 2009, which Murray won 2-6, 6-3, 6-3, 5-7, 6-3.

Bibliography

BOOKS

Barrett, John, *Wimbledon The Official History Of The Championships* (London: Collins Willow, 2001)

Becker, Boris with Robert Lübenoff and Helmut Sorge, *The Player* (London: Bantam Press, 2004)

Block, Maxine (Ed), *Current Biography 1941* (New York: H.W. Wilson, 1941)

Bodo, Pete, *Ashe Vs Connors Wimbledon 1975: Tennis That Went Beyond Centre Court* (London: Aurum, 2015)

Bradford, Sarah, *George VI* (London: Penguin, 2011)

Brown, Cameron, *Wimbledon Facts, Figures & Fun* (London: FF&F, 2005)

Collins, Bud, *The Bud Collins History Of Tennis* (3rd Ed) (Chicago: New Chapter Press, 2016)

Conner, Floyd, *Tennis's Most Wanted* (Washington DC, Brassey's, 2002)

Deford, Frank, *Big Bill Tilden The Triumphs And The Tragedy* (London: Victor Gollancz, 1977)

Evert Lloyd, Chris with Neil Amdur, *Chrissie* (London: New English Library, 1983)

Ferguson, Norman, *Sports Scandals* (Chichester: Summersdale, 2016)

Garraty, John A. (Ed), *Dictionary Of American Biography Supplement Five 1951-1955* (New York: Charles Scribner's Sons, 1977)

    – and Mark C. Carnes (Eds) *Dictionary Of American Biography Supplement Eight 1966-1970* (New York: Charles Scribner's Sons, 1988)

    – *American National Biography* (New York: Oxford University Press, 1999)

Grasso, John, *Historical Dictionary Of Tennis* (Lanham, Maryland, The Scarecrow Press: 2011)

James, Edward T. (Ed), *Dictionary Of American Biography Supplement Three 1941-1945* (New York: Charles Scribner's Sons, 1973)

Kane, Joseph Nathan, Steven Anzovin and Janet Podell, *Famous First Facts* (New York: H.W. Wilson, 2006)

King, Billie Jean with Frank Deford, *The Autobiography Of Billie Jean King* (London: Granada Publishing, 1983)

Matthew, H.C.G. and Brian Harrison (Eds), *Oxford Dictionary Of National Biography* (Oxford: Oxford University Press, 2004)

McEnroe, John, *But Seriously, An Autobiography* (London: Weidenfeld & Nicolson, 2018)

Moritz, Charles (Ed), *Current Biography Yearbook 1963* (New York: H.W. Wilson, 1964)

Myers, Wallis, A. *Captain Anthony Wilding* (London: Hodder & Stoughton, 1916)

Nairn, Bede and Geoffrey Serle (Eds), *Australian Dictionary Of Biography Volume 7 1891-1939* (Melbourne: Melbourne University Press, 1979)

O'Neal, Tatum, *A Paper Life* (New York: Harper Entertainment, 2004)

Perry, Fred, *An Autobiography* (London: Arrow Books, 1975)

Pryor, Sean, *McEnroe Superman Or Superbrat?* (London: Star Books, 1982)

Ritchie, John (Ed), *Australian Dictionary Of Biography Volume 13 1940-1980* (Melbourne: Melbourne University Press, 1993)

Robertson, Patrick, *The Guinness Book Of Australian Firsts* (Melbourne: Guinness Books/Collins Australia, 1987)

—— *Robertson's Book Of Firsts* (New York: Bloomsbury, 2011)

Rothe, Anne (Ed), *Current Biography 1951* (New York: H.W. Wilson, 1952)

Seddon, Peter, *Tennis's Strangest Matches* (London: Robson Books, 2001)

Serle, Geoffrey (Ed), *Australian Dictionary Of Biography Volume 11 1891-1939* (Melbourne: Melbourne University Press, 1988)

Tingay, Lance, *The Guinness Book Of Tennis Facts And Feats* (Middlesex: Guinness, 1983)

Walker, Randy, *On this Day In Tennis History* (Chicago: New Chapter Press, 2008)

Wallace, Irving, Amy Wallace, David Wallechinsky and Sylvia Wallace, *The Intimate Sex Lives Of Famous People* (Port Townsend, Washington: Feral House, 2008)

Wallechinsky, David and Jaime Loucky, *The Complete Book Of The Olympics* (London: Aurum, 2012)

– *The Complete Book Of The Winter Olympics* (London: Aurum, 2006)

MAGAZINES
Sports Illustrated
The Atlantic

NEWSPAPERS
Daily Mirror
Pittsburgh Post-Gazette
Sarasota Journal
Sydney Morning Herald
The Age
The Glasgow Herald
The Guardian
The Independent
The New York Times
The Times
The Toledo Blade

WEBSITES
http://adb.anu.edu.au
https://www.atptour.com
https://blackamericaweb.com
https://www.daviscup.com
en.wikipedia.org
https://www.herald.ie/
https://kooyong.com.au
http://www.myjacobfamily.com
https://www.rolandgarros.com
https://www.sports-reference.com/
https://www.statenislandcc.org/
https://www.tennisarchives.com
https://www.tennisforum.com
http://www.tennis-histoire.com
https://thewestsidetennisclub.com/